James Edward McGee

Lives of Irishmen's sons and their descendants

James Edward McGee

Lives of Irishmen's sons and their descendants

ISBN/EAN: 9783744741118

Printed in Europe, USA, Canada, Australia, Japan

Cover: Foto ©ninafisch / pixelio.de

More available books at **www.hansebooks.com**

MARSHAL McMAHON.

LIVES

OF

IRISHMEN'S SONS

AND

THEIR DESCENDANTS.

BY

COLONEL JAMES E. McGEE,

AUTHOR OF "IRISH SOLDIERS IN EVERY LAND."

NEW YORK:
J. A. McGEE, PUBLISHER,
7 BARCLAY ST.

1874.

Entered, according to Act of Congress, April, 1874,
By JAMES E. MCGEE,
In the office of the Librarian of Congress, at Washington, D. C,

Printed and Stereotyped at the New York Catholic Protectory,
West Chester, New York.

TO MY YOUNG FELLOW-CITIZENS

BORN IN AMERICA

OF

IRISH DESCENT OR PARENTAGE,

HOPING, WHILE THEY WILL PROVE LOYAL TO THE

LAND OF THEIR BIRTH,

THEY WILL NOT BE FOUND WANTING IN LOVE AND

ESTEEM FOR THAT OF THEIR

FOREFATHERS,

THIS VOLUME IS AFFECTIONATELY

DEDICATED

BY THE AUTHOR.

PREFACE.

In selecting the lives of five great men as the subjects of this volume, I had the following objects in view:

I. I thought I perceived in their histories the development of as many distinct types of Irish character, widely differing one from the other, but all exhibiting in a remarkable degree, the national, latent genius of our race, modified by time, place, and circumstances. McMahon, Duke of Magenta and President of the French Republic, has long seemed to me the *beau idéal* of a Franco-Irish soldier; brave, austere, and reserved, loving arms as a profession and his native country with his whole heart, yet capable of yielding at times to the softer impulses of our nature, or of leading a desperate charge, amid dead and dying, with undisturbed composure. Andrew Jackson, seventh President of our Republic, I regard as a thorough North-of-Ireland Gael; rugged, inflexible, and thoroughly tenacious in purpose, with a mind that arrived at just conclusions more by intuition than through reflection, and whose will was so unswerving that he easily gained the mastery over more cultivated, but less firm dispositions. The late Cardinal Wiseman was the lineal descendant, in the spiritual order, of those devoted and learned men, who in the infancy of the Church in the West, gave to Ireland the proud title of the Isle of Scholars and Saints, and whose missionary labors were circumscribed only by the bounds of the then known world. His Spanish birth and Roman education may have somewhat tempered and refined his natural idiosyncrasies, but, in almost all his actions may be traced that ardent love for learning, and burning zeal in the propagation of the faith, which characterized the disciples of St. Patrick and their successors.

General Sheridan is the modern Irish soldier, very little changed by his American associations, and might, if he had been born a couple of centuries ago, have ridden beside Owen Roe, or charged with Patrick Sarsfield. Fieldmarshal O'Donnell, on the other hand, may be regarded as among the last of a race of men who in former times swayed much more by their physical, mental, and social qualities than by any hereditary right. Ardently devoted to the profession of arms, princely in generosity and lavish in expenditure, of unsullied personal honor, they looked upon their swords as the insignia of the highest nobility, and the field of battle as the true stage for the exhibition of all their many virtues. They have nearly all passed away, but though the world may have grown wiser and less romantic, it cannot recall their chivalrous deeds without a sympathetic sigh.

II. Of late years it has become the fashion with a certain class of political speakers, and editors of obscure newspapers, who, wishing to trade on the generous instincts of the Irish immigrants in America, think to flatter their vanity by claiming as Irish every man of Gaelic nomenclature, regardless of where he was born or what have been his antecedents. This is neither correct nor complimentary to those to whom such assertions are addressed, and, if honestly entertained, simply defeats the ends sought to be attained. McMahon, for example, is not an Irishman but a Frenchman, as Jackson was a true type of an American democrat, who loved Tennessee much better than he did Antrim. Those who claim too much will not even be accorded what is their due. I was anxious, therefore, in part at least, to correct this growing and, to me, humiliating evil, by placing before the public a few great names, not as Irishmen, but as the inheritors of the brain and muscle of that undying race from which so many distinguished men have sprung, developed and trained by foreign associations, as well as by the accident of birth.

III. I was also desirous to show to those who, not caring to look under the surface of society, or to trace the connection between cause and effect, frequently ask why it is that Ireland does not now produce more great thinkers, scientific soldiers, and astute statesmen, that the reason is the expatriation of that class of her population which produces the clearest minds and the most acute understandings. This emigration found an outlet on the continent of Europe in the last century, and left as its descendants such men as the Duke of Magenta and the Cardinal Archbishop of Westminster. Later, the tide was turned to the Western World, and, disappearing gradually in the course of nature, left behind as its representatives such men as Jackson and Sheridan. Had Ireland enjoyed the advantages of an independent, paternal government, the greater part of her children would have still nestled lovingly in her bosom, and the valor, learning, and genius which have been lavished by her sons and their offspring in every part of the globe, would have been cherished and nurtured at home.

IV. If I have succeeded in effecting any of these objects, or even in suggesting their accomplishment to others, I shall be well satisfied, trusting that as time passes and correct ideas of contemporary characters become more general, the mental gifts and meritorious actions of the descendants of the Irish in this, as in other lands, will be found as conspicuous and praiseworthy as those of any other race now represented among us.

J. E. M.

NEW YORK, January, 1874.

CONTENTS.

	PAGE
McMahon, Duke of Magenta, President of France	11
Andrew Jackson, Seventh President of the United States	67
Cardinal Nicholas Wiseman	155
Lieutenant-General Philip H. Sheridan	212
Fieldmarshal Leopold O'Donnell, Count of Lucena and Duke of Tetuan	262

IRISHMEN'S SONS.

McMAHON, DUKE OF MAGENTA,

PRESIDENT OF FRANCE.

As we write, one of the foremost men in Christendom, as far certainly as reputation, abilities, position, and all that constitutes mundane greatness are concerned, is undoubtedly MARIA ESME PATRICK MAURICE MCMAHON, the highest ranking officer in the French army, and, for the time being at least, president of the French Republic.

This remarkable man was born in the old family mansion at Sully, France, on the 13th day of June, 1808. Though not of immediate Irish parentage, there is no possible doubt that paternally he is the direct descendant of a very ancient and noble Irish family, and can trace his pedigree in a direct line through successive generations for at least five hundred years. Patrick McMahon, a more modern ancestor, was an officer in King James II's army and a native of Torrodile, county Limerick, Ireland. Upon the defeat of that unfortunate monarch's forces he left the country and, with his wife Margaret, *née* O'Sullivan, and his children, emigrated to France and took service under Louis XIV. One of his sons, John McMahon, also a soldier, was created first Count d'Equilly for distinguished and meritorious conduct. Though brought up in France, D'Equilly seems not only to have been a loyal French subject but an ardent Irishman proud of his name and race, and not ashamed of his native land in the hour of her humiliation. We find from an examination of the archives of Birmingham Tower, Dublin, that on September 28th, 1749, he applied by letter to the authorities of that day to have all historical and genealogical papers and records connected with the history of his family, collected, collated, and recorded, and official copies of the same forwarded to him, "so that his children and his posterity in France might know that they were of Irish descent." As he accompanied this request with a liberal fee, it is unnecessary to say it was granted. This patriotic Count was the grandfather of the present Marshal, Duke and President.

But Patrick McMahon seems to have had other children, for in 1760, a petition was sent to Louis XV, from Captain Maurice McMahon, a Knight of Malta, on behalf of himself and of his brothers, Count d'Equilly and the Bishop of Killaloe, setting forth, among other matters, that "they draw their maternal origin from the lords of Clondirola, in Ireland, who were descended from the lords and princes of Clare, who were issue of the ancient monarchs of Ireland. Their attachment to the Catholic religion and their legitimate prince have deprived them of their possessions and titles, and they find it impossible to establish their noble and ancient extraction by literal proofs. But they have proofs and testimonials beyond all suspicion, and admitted by the tribunals, which establish their nobility, not only from the year 1400, but even up to Brian Boru, monarch of Ireland in the beginning of the eleventh century, and that they are of the same family as the Earls of Thomond, whom the king has honored with his favor." We are not informed what was the effect of this appeal, and we have no doubt of its veracity, but from the character of the effete sovereign who then disgraced the throne of France, we conclude that it was thrown aside and forgotten.

The number of the D'Equilly family we have no means of ascertaining, but it is certain that he gave at least two sons to the service of his adopted country: one, the second count of the name, the father of the subject of our sketch, who rose to the rank of Lieutenant-General, and Commander of the Royal and Military Order of St. Louis, and the other a younger brother who attained the position of Major-General.

With such family antecedents and with

the hereditary military genius of his race, it required little foresight to prognosticate a brilliant future for the cherished scion of the house of McMahon-D'Equilly. His father certainly, with natural parental affection, appears to have indulged in such fond anticipations, and to have paid the most scrupulous attention to his education, physical, mental, and moral. His first studies were made under the supervision of his parents at a quiet preparatory school in Autun, which he left for the Military Academy of St. Cyr in November, 1825, being then in his seventeenth year.

It was previous to this event that he acquired a knowledge of those cardinal principles which were destined to form a character so remarkable, and to govern his entire life. Abstinence, self-denial of all deleterious pleasures, and vigorous exercise, built up a constitution that seems to have defied the ravages of climate, exposure, and time itself; quiet communings with his father beneath the shade of his ancestral forests gave to his disposition a serious, though by no means sombre coloring, while that deep reverence for religion, that love for the faith of his fathers, which have ever characterized him, were nurtured and matured at his mother's knee, and in the society of his friends and relatives.

St. Cyr, it is generally known, is not only one of the best military colleges in existence, but it is, and was, particularly after the restoration of Louis XVIII, one of the most aristocratic and sociably most exclusive. Thither what has been called the best blood of France, the descendants of the Montmorencis, Maurepas, Cavaignacs, De Broglies, and even the princes of the royal blood, were sent to learn the rudiments of that art, in the practice of which so many of them have shed such lustre on their order and on the gallant nation they in part represented.

In less than two years young McMahon completed his course, to the entire satisfaction of his professors, and left St. Cyr with an excellent reputation as a student and the rank of *sous-lieutenant élève,* having been assigned to the 4th Huzzars, in which an older brother was already captain.

In 1830, however, upon the resignation of the latter, the young soldier, anxious to experience the excitement and danger of actual warfare, of which he had been only enjoying "the pomp, pride, and circumstance," exchanged into the 20th regiment and embarked with it for Algeria, then the theatre of hazardous and continuous conflict. Still we may presume that the years of peace were not misspent by the future Fieldmarshal, for on emerging from St. Cyr and his entry into the service, he joined the Staff School of Instruction, in which all the time that could be spared from his routine duties was employed. Scott, in his "Military Dictionary," lays it down as an axiom that the staff officer should at least know as much as the General whom he serves. Artillery practice, cavalry and infantry tactics, and strategy are the least of his attainments; familiarity with permanent and field fortifications; topographical engineering and surveying; drawing, designing, and map-making; means of supply and transportation, and the knowledge of a hundred other details affecting the organization, movement, equipment, and disposition of troops in quarters or on the march, form the most essential qualifications of an accomplished *aide*.

Three years diligently spent in the acquisition of these multitudinous branches of the military profession must have produced a marked effect on a mind so peculiarly constituted as that of the young *sous-lieutenant*, for even at that early age he was preëminent for his sedate habits, unostentatious industry, and application, as well as for his extraordinary capacity for mastering the most abstruse scientific problems. His tastes led him naturally toward the higher branches, such as mathematics and astronomy, the study of which generally has a tendency to give system and steadiness to the reasoning faculties, as well as to elevate the mind above the little affairs of life; while his innate pride and gravity of character prevented him from taking part in the frivolities and dissipation too often indulged in by his junior brother officers.

Thus, after five years' training in St. Cyr and the Staff School, at the green age of twenty-two we find the young Franco-Irish soldier, enthusiastic though self-contained, entering on his career of danger and glory, thoroughly versed in the theory of warfare, and only anxious to submit his school knowledge to the test of actual experience. On his arrival in Algeria he was detached from the 20th and placed on the staff of General Achard, then commanding the French forces in Africa. As orderly officer to that commander he formed a portion of his personal staff, and accompanied him on his first expedition against Medeah. On this his "first brush" he greatly distinguished himself, it is said, by his coolness and intrepidity in bearing despatches from one part of the lines to another, under the fire of a keen and skilful enemy, always on the alert to pick off their opponents in gross or in detail. Belidah is mentioned as one of the scenes of his gallantry, when the future stormer of the Malakoff, being alone, was closely pursued by a body of Arabs, who shot his horse under him and nearly ended his military aspirations forever.

General Achard was the next year recalled and sent into the Low Countries. He took with him his favorite staff-officer, who is mentioned in contemporaneous reports as having exhibited his usual bravery and self-possession at the siege of Antwerp in 1832, during the Belgian revolution. For his conduct on this occasion he was promoted to a captaincy and decorated with the insignia of the Order of St. Leopold.

As the war in Africa at that time does not appear to have been prosecuted with any degree of vigor, or to have presented many opportunities for preferment or distinction—the soldier's twin guiding stars—Captain McMahon did not return to Algeria till 1836, when affairs seemed about to assume a more earnest and, to him, a more interesting aspect. He was at once attached to the staff of General Damremont, and in the desperate assault on the city and fortifications of Constantine was, as might have been expected, conspicuous for his efficiency and daring. This time, however, he did not come out of the struggle scathless, for during that engagement of almost unparalleled fierceness between the instruments of aggressive civilization and the wild children of the desert, who strove to defend their homes and families, he was badly wounded and obliged to be taken off the field. Yet his sufferings were, in his opinion, more than amply solaced by his being appointed an officer of the Legion of Honor. France, whether monarchical, imperialistic, or republican, always knew how to reward her soldiers.

Upon recovering from his injuries and again reporting for duty, McMahon was assigned to General Changarnier's staff, a position which he occupied until 1840, when a wider field and a more responsible career were opened to him. In that year the *Chasseurs-à-pied*, or as they were sometimes called the *Chasseurs d'Orléans*, after their organizer, the prince of that name, were raised for African service, and the command of the tenth battalion having been tendered to McMahon, it was accepted. Heretofore he had acted only on the staff, endeavoring by practical observation and strict obedience to learn how to command. He was now, at the age of thirty-two, to have an independent force—a flying column as it were—and a miniature staff of his own.

In the two years following, at the head of his chasseurs he made several successful incursions into the country of the Kabyles, and took an active part in the decisive campaign which eventuated in the complete subjugation of the Arab tribes, and the capture of their great chief Abd-el-Kader.

His promotion now became rapid, and must have been highly satisfactory to the distinguished soldier who, as a sous-lieutenant had, more than a decade past, evinced so much youthful bravery combined with mature deliberation and knowledge of his profession. In 1842, he was commissioned Lieutenant-Colonel in the 2d Foreign Legion, next, Colonel of the 41st Infantry, and finally, in 1848, Brigadier-General. His semi-civic advancement also showed what confidence was placed in his prudence and executive abilities by the government of the day, for in the latter year we find him Governor of Tiemeen, and in the following, his jurisdiction was extended over the provinces of Constantine and Oran.

But greater honors awaited him. In July, 1852, he was promoted General of Division, and while yet engaged in subduing the Algerine tribes and endeavoring to bring those already conquered under some regular system of government, the Crimean war, as it is called, broke out in 1854, when he was summoned to France to take part in it. McMahon was assigned at once to the command of the First *corps d'armée*, and, with a portion of the Allied fleet, ordered to the Baltic, the intention being that, after the reduction of Cronstadt by the naval forces, a landing of the troops should be effected, and by thus threatening the capital to make a powerful diversion in favor of the southern movement. The attempt failed. Cronstadt was found so strongly fortified as to be unassailable; the British went through the forms of an attack and retired, and the whole project was abandoned. In consequence of this, McMahon's sphere of action was transferred to the still famous peninsula of Chersonese, so renowned in ancient military as well as legendary history.

Whatever may be thought of the motives or causes which led to that war, it cannot well be denied that the Colossus of the North, semi-civilized though it was and is to this day, but more decidedly so twenty years ago, displayed in its struggle with the Western powers, immense resources, great administrative ability, endurance, bravery, and even genius. Attacking Turkey at her own doors, and threatening

England's Asiatic possessions, Russia necessarily aroused the hostility of some of the most powerful and martial nations of southwestern Europe, who, combining their maritime, military, and moneyed resources against her, seemed about, by one decisive blow, not only to check her career of conquest but to destroy, utterly ruin, and disintegrate the gigantic but ill-cemented mass which constitutes the Muscovite Empire. Had Austria then joined the quadruple alliance, it is not improbable that such a comprehensive scheme would have been carried out, but that astute power held aloof, preferring to see her rivals engaged in weakening each other; and her neutrality, as may be seen at a glance at the map of Europe, left Russia vulnerable only on two sides: by the Baltic and the Black seas.

The approach by the former, however, was beset by many and almost insurmountable difficulties. Every defensible point was strongly fortified; while nature, far mightier than man in her works, had closed up the ocean itself for more than six months in the year by an icy barrier more impassable than moat or castle wall. The attempt, therefore, in this direction to assail a vital part of the empire, if even seriously contemplated, failed, and the main movement had to be directed against the southern extremity of the Czar's dominions, the Crimea.

Sebastopol, the principal position and key to the peninsula, was at that time and, notwithstanding the ravages of war, continues to be, a place of great natural strength. Its harbor, partly the work of art, is capacious and deep, and susceptible of having its approaches strongly defended from the surrounding eminences. Before the war, its docks, hewn out of the solid rock, were regarded as triumphs of engineering skill, and its extensive dockyards were capable of turning out annually, not only large fleets of merchandise, but of supplying the government with all the armed ships it required to carry its flag into every part in the Black and Azof seas. Large stores of ordnance, small arms, powder, and other munitions of war were kept continually in the arsenals, while a garrison of more than ordinary magnitude was stationed constantly in its fortifications to defend the position and keep the heterogeneous population in awe and order.

It was against this place, at once a fortress and a naval rendezvous, that the whole force of the powers that had declared war against Russia was directed. England provided the largest naval armament and a very respectable military force, the greater part of which was, unfortunately, composed of Irishmen, twenty thousand of whom embarked from Dublin for the intended seat of war early in 1854, and only three thousand of whom returned after two years' service. France furnished a most imposing army but a smaller fleet. Italy, or rather Sardinia, sent twenty thousand land-forces, while Turkey's quota consisted principally of bands of irregular cavalry, and infantry still more barbarous, and fanatical scouts, thieves, and licentious marauders. Taken altogether, it was a mighty and varied host, and had one element of success at least, a spirit of national rivalry. At the outset, the commander-in-chief was Lord Raglan, but his successors were all Frenchmen. Of course, during the progress of the war each country kept the depleted ranks of its armies as full as possible by recruiting at home, but as we are not aware that any reliable returns of the grand total have ever been published, it is impossible to say with accuracy how many men, ships, and guns were operating against the enemy.

On the side of Russia, from the meagre accounts received, generally through hostile channels, we conclude that there were about two hundred thousand men of all arms, and as their lines of communication had been cut early in the struggle and their fleet sunk and destroyed to prevent its capture, there is no reason to believe that any considerable reinforcements reached them during the siege. It has also been stated upon apparently good authority, that before the approach of Raglan in rear of the city, the fortifications on that side were very weak, and bore no comparison whatever to those afterwards erected in front of the Allies under the intelligent superintendence of Totleben.

The first serious battle between the contending armies was that of the Alma, September 20, 1854, which was gained by the Allies under command of Fieldmarshal Leroy de St. Arnaud, who had succeeded Lord Raglan, and who himself in a few days afterwards gave place to Pélissier. General McMahon, who on his arrival in the Crimea was ordered to relieve Canrobert in the command of the first division of the second corps of the French contingent, doubtless took an active part in this action. Then followed the engagements of Balaclava and Inkermann, after the latter of which the Russians withdrew behind their newly-made fortifications, and sullenly prepared for a regular and long siege.

This lasted through the terrible winter of 1854-'55, and into the autumn of the latter year, all the hideous features of an investment—famine, pestilence, and death—exhibiting themselves as prominently to the besiegers as to the beleaguered. Of the English army alone ten thousand are said to have died from want or exposure, though the French, having a better commissariat, did not suffer so severely from those causes.

At length, in September, 1855, it was resolved to make a general attack on the entire works, the principal of which were the Malakoff and the Redan, the Mamelon Vert having been destroyed some time previously. Of the two remaining, the Malakoff, it is known, was immeasurably the strongest and largest, and its capture, according to military courtesy, was assigned by the French commander-in-chief to his own countrymen, while the English and Italian troops were directed against the minor work. To General McMahon was intrusted the desperate and hazardous, but, to the true soldier, the highly honorable duty of leading the assault.

About noon on the 7th of September, the Russian garrison was surprised to see, during a lull in the firing, a mass of French soldiers swarming up the slope in their front, some in solid column of attack, and others, the *tirailleurs* and zouaves, scattered over the entire surface without any apparent order. The very audacity of the manœuvre for awhile silenced the men within the defences, but their inaction was momentary. Every gun that could be brought to bear on the assailants belched forth its deadly missiles, and volleys from ten thousand muskets swelled the awful din. Many of the French troops fell at the first fire, but their movements had been so well designed and so swiftly executed that before a second or third discharge could be given they were across the dikes, over the *chevaux-de-frise*, in through the embrasures and upon the ramparts. Then ensued a desperate hand-to-hand encounter in the trenches seldom equalled in the magnitude of the number engaged or in the obstinacy with which every inch of ground was disputed. For a time the result seemed doubtful, and even Pélissier, fearing the works were mined, sent word to McMahon that it was best to retire. His reply was characteristic: *J'y suis entré, et j'y resterai.* Gradually the Russians gave way before the impetuosity and desperate gallantry of their Gallic foemen, and finally their retreat from the works, at first stern and orderly, became changed into a precipitate and confused rout. Thus was the great Malakoff won and the city of Sebastopol virtually captured.

But while this terrible drama was being enacted on one part of the field, another, of a very different character, was presented at no great distance. The English and their Italian auxiliaries had recoiled from the fire of the Redan, and lay cowering in the zigzags, in some cases refusing to obey their officers who, to do them all justice, were anxious to make another attempt to capture the fort. McMahon saw the difficulty at once, and promptly turning the captured guns of the Malakoff on its sister work, so overawed its defenders that under cover of his fire the English again assaulted and entered the trenches with little trouble. The entire defences being now in possession of the Allies, the defeated army, under cover of the night, withdrew in good order, the city proper surrendered, and the war, for all practical purposes, ended.

For his gallant conduct on this occasion General McMahon received the Grand Cross of the Legion of Honor; he had already at intervals been decorated with the insignia of the inferior grades, with the political rank of Senator of France, and, what he probably most valued, the highest encomiums of his brother officers and the applause of the entire nation. It is a strange coincidence that the very theatre of his glory in this instance should have been in the country which more than a century previous had been won for Russia by the compatriot and fellow soldier of his grandfather, Field-marshal Lacy.

The treaty of Paris, which followed soon after the fall of Sebastopol, restored peace to Europe, so McMahon's services were again transferred to Algeria. He was made commander-in-chief of the land and naval forces of that province, but, though constantly engaged with one or other of the wild tribes of that irrepressible region, we do not find any incident in his career worth recording till the Franco-Italian war of 1859 again brought him prominently before the world and crowned him with new laurels.

Early in that year the Emperor Napoleon, in conjunction with the King of Sardinia, prepared to drive Austria from her possessions in Northern Italy, and, in the cant phrase of the day, to proclaim the "unification" of the Italian peninsula. In the spring he accordingly departed from admiring and enthusiastic France with a large and splendidly equipped army, in which General McMahon commanded the Second Corps. On the 21st of May the first collision between the contending forces took place at Montebello, in which fifteen thousand Austrians were defeated by the advance guard of the French. Then followed a short, sharp, and brilliant campaign, and a succession of battles the description of which recalls to our minds the lightning-like movements of the first Napoleon in his youthful and more successful days. Palestro, May 30; Magenta, June 4; Malignano, June 18; Solferino, June 24, were a series of victorious encounters with an enemy, if not of equal numbers, which is doubtful, certainly not inferior in skill, bravery, and knowledge of the country. In two months from the date of the declaration of war the treaty of Villafranca was signed, and the map of southern Europe materially changed. While Venetia remained to Austria, Lombardy was annexed to Sardinia, and soon after Nice and Savoy became an integral portion of France.

In this campaign, so dazzling in its inception and execution and so pregnant of future results, Napoleon III and Victor Emmanuel were of course merely the nominal commanders, Pélissier, McMahon, and other distinguished general officers, planning and carrying out to ultimate triumph all the strategic and tactical movements of the allied armies. The latter's first great achievement on Italian soil took place on the 4th of June. On that day the main body of the Franco-Italian army, under the immediate command of the Emperor, attacked the Austrians, then strongly entrenched around the village and bridge of Magenta. The numbers on either side were about equal, from one hundred and fifty thousand to one hundred and eighty thousand. The struggle was long and obstinate, and at one time dire defeat stared the Allies in the face, when suddenly a French force appeared on the left, marching hastily to the support of their comrades. As the grand column approached the scene of doubtful combat it deployed in mass, and sweeping down on the astonished Austrians, scattered them in all directions and changed anticipated victory into utter rout. This was McMahon's command, led by himself in person. The day previously he had left Novara, it is credibly said without orders, and rapidly passing through Turbigo and Buffalora, arrived on the field of Magenta just in time to change the fortunes of the day and save the honor of the French arms.

The losses on this occasion, as is the case in accounts of most battles, have never been accurately known, but those of the Austrians, not including prisoners, are generally set down at five thousand, and of the Allies at about three-fifths of that number.

For his timely, judicious, and unlooked-for aid the French emperor was deeply and naturally grateful, and expressed to McMahon on the field orally and afterwards in general orders, his high appreciation of the services he had rendered to the army and to France. Subsequently he created him Fieldmarshal and Duke of Magenta.

On the 24th of the same month another and a more decisive victory was gained at Solferino. Three hundred and fifty thousand men are said to have been engaged on both sides, and the final result of the battle having been anticipated as decisive, no matter upon which side victory inclined, it was fought with remarkable intrepidity and determination. On this occasion the Austrians took the offensive. On the morning of that eventful day, although occupying a very strong position, they did not wait the onset of the Allies, but, crossing the river Chiese, fell with such fury on the Franco-Italians as to drive back both wings, the left, composed of the Sardinians under Victor Emmanuel, being the first to give way. At this crisis the rout of the whole army seemed imminent, and doubtless would have been so had the Austrians restrained their ardor and had, instead of pushing their advantage too far against the broken wings, taken the French centre on both flanks and so crushed it between two fires. The error thus committed was speedily taken advantage of by Pélissier and McMahon, who, concentrating all their forces, attacked the Austrian centre and utterly destroyed it. This was the turning point of the engagement. The Austrian army hastily retreated over the Chiese in as good order as could be expected, leaving, however, in the hands of the victors thirty guns, three flags, and about seven thousand prisoners. The losses on both sides were heavy, and are thus stated: Sardinia, two hundred and sixteen officers and four thousand and fifty-one non-commissioned officers and privates killed or wounded, and twelve hundred and twenty-eight missing; total, five thousand five hundred and twenty-five. France, seven hundred and fifty officers (including five Generals wounded, seven colonels and six lieutenant-colonels killed) and twelve thousand enlisted men killed or wounded. Austria, seventeen thousand officers and men killed, wounded, or prisoners.

McMahon's services on this day were of the same efficient character as usual, and, though only second in actual command, contributed materially to the success of the Allies. It is said, on reliable authority, that it was he who suggested the concentrated attack on the Austrian centre which virtually decided the combat, and it is certain that in person at the head of his corps he stormed and took the fortified heights which stretched from Cavriano to Medolo, the enemy's strongest position. Those hills, bristling with batteries as they were, had heretofore been considered impregnable, but to a soldier who could take a Malakoff before dinner they did not present very serious obstacles. But even the marshal's bravery and skill at this battle paled before his actions at Magenta. His praises had been already sounded, not only in France but throughout Europe, and in Italy especially the mention of his name evoked the warmest praise and the wildest enthusiasm.

The treaty of Villafranca, as we have seen, followed speedily on the victory of Solferino; peace once more spread her dove-like wings over the nations of Europe, and the conquerors returned home to receive the congratulations of their countrymen and to wear their well-won honors, some in quietude and retirement, others in the public service. Of the latter was the Duke of Magenta, who seems never to have tired of devoting his genius, large experience, and high character to the public good. When the present Emperor of Germany was crowned King of Prussia in 1861, he was deputed by Napoleon as special envoy to represent France at Berlin, a duty which he performed to the great satisfaction and gratification of both courts. Shortly after he relieved Canrobert in the command of the Third Corps, and in 1864 we again find him in Algeria as Governor-General, a position he soon after resigned and again returned to France.

We now come to an epoch in the gallant marshal's life which belongs more to the domain of contemporary history than to that of biography. Hitherto we have followed him step by step in the paths of undimmed glory and uninterrupted success. We have found the untitled young *sous-lieutenant* winning his way to a marshal's bâton, the Grand Cross of the Legion of Honor, a senatorship, and a dukedom, by a course of unswerving devotion to his profession and his country, ever in the van of danger and always victorious. We have now to behold him, for awhile, outnumbered, defeated, and if not betrayed, certainly basely deceived. The history of the late Franco-German war is not written, nor will even a tittle of the secret motives and designs which led to it, and the underhand means taken to conduct it to its disastrous termination, ever be known. Even as we write the actual commander-in-chief of the French force is on trial for his life, charged with incapacity, duplicity, and treason, and the evidence so far produced from some of the highest ranking officers in his late command, and from ministers of state, leaves on the mind a painful impression that the charges are not without some foundation.

Still there are some general facts connected with the Franco-German war which have been stated with such clearness, and confirmed by results so striking, that they have received general credence. It is now known that for a long time, two or three years at least, Prussia had been preparing for an aggressive war on France; that her armies had been put on a most efficient war footing, equipped in the newest style, and armed with the most approved weapons; that France, up to the gates of Paris, and even Paris itself, had been carefully surveyed, and everything noted, from a first-class fort to a pigsty; and that everywhere in the threatened sections swarmed German spies, in one garb or another, as laborers, clerks, and even subordinate *attachés* of the French bureaux. The pretence, then, of Kaiser William, that he was forced into a war, may be considered a flimsy diplomatic falsehood, and his insult to the French ambassador, which nominally led to the beginning of hostilities, a mere piece of chicanery.

France, on the other hand, was not blameless, and in the minds of many who sincerely sympathize with her, deserved the abject humiliation inflicted by her ancient enemy. Elated beyond bounds by the brilliant successes of the Italian campaign, the officers of the French armies, as a general thing, became self-sufficient, careless, and, as a consequence, ignorant of their duties and disinclined to perform them with that military regularity which is so essential to the efficiency of all armies. They were more at home in the boudoir and the billiard saloon than in the barrack or on the drill ground, and the consequence was that, when suddenly called into active service, they were found unprepared, either to endure the hardships of a campaign or "fight their men" with any degree of skill, or, what is the result only of skill and courage combined, coolness and precision. Then again the late emperor, Napoleon III, allowed himself to be grossly deceived as to the number of available men and munitions of war at his disposal, by a set of dishonest quartermasters, commissaries, and others, whose duty it was to make regular reports of the condition of the army, but who, by swelling its numbers on paper and reporting the purchase of military stores that had no existence, contrived in a short time to enrich themselves at the expense of the nation. That the French emperor, otherwise so far-seeing and astute, should have allowed himself to have been so long misled and should have plunged into a war without accurate knowledge of his strength and resources, was not only astonishing but little short of criminal; and though he in some measure personally paid the penalty of his credulity, it will be a long time before the nation he once governed can heal the wounds and forget the shame inflicted on her through his incapacity.

While France was vaporing about her "natural boundary, the Rhine," and doing nothing but boasting, Prussia, who not only wished to create and consolidate a German empire, but to annex Alsace and Lorraine, a large portion of the population of which, of German descent and speaking that language, are poetically considered part of the Fatherland. Accordingly the declaration of war had scarcely been promulgated when every road and avenue leading across the frontier into the coveted provinces was thronged with armed men, guns, wagons, and ambulances. So quick was the movement, so complete the previous preparations, that it may well be said that before Napoleon set out from Paris the Germans had possession of nearly every strategical position on the French frontier, their line of communication with their base of supplies being at the same time open and unassailable.

The Emperor did set out at last to take command of his army, but it would have been much better for his reputation and for France if he had remained in his capital, and allowed his veteran officers to conduct the war. Experience has shown that mere nominal commanders are potent only for evil. The army was in two divisions, the first under Bazaine, and the other commanded by McMahon. The headquarters were fixed at Metz, a very strongly fortified town, susceptible of still further defences. On the 2d of July, 1871, Marshal McMahon, with a force of about forty thousand, was ordered in an easterly and forward direction to make a recognizance in force, and having proceeded as far as Woerth he suddenly found himself confronted by the enemy, estimated at one hundred and sixty thousand men, under the personal supervision of the Crown Prince of Prussia. In obeying his orders he necessarily became separated from the main body of the army, and being vastly outnumbered and partly surrounded, his position was a desperate one. To fight against such odds was his only course, and this he did without much hesitation. The unequal conflict lasted nearly all day and the havoc on both sides was proportionally great. The Marshal was in every part of the field, urging on and encouraging, in person, his men, while at the same time he paid particular attention to his wings, which were several times in danger of being outflanked by their more numerous opponents. Occasionally the French, by the precision of their artillery fire, or the impetuosity of their infantry charges, would drive back the Germans, but only for a moment, for the depleted ranks were soon reinforced, and the fight renewed. In vain McMahon, his staff-officers disabled and his horse shot, rode into the very heart of the conflict, the immensely superior force of the Crown Prince was gradually closing round him and threatened to cut him off from Metz, and even capture his entire command. Under cover of night he took the only step that could present itself to a judicious general. He retreated on Paris, with the intention of uniting himself with the large body of troops collected there under Trochu, hoping that thus, while covering the capital, he would soon be strong enough to advance and, if necessary, form a junction with Bazaine.

The war department, however, in their self-sufficient wisdom ordained otherwise. Hearing of his approach they sent him orders to march to Metz forthwith, but neglected to send him a man or a gun by way of reinforcing his crippled column. As was his wont he obeyed his instructions to the letter, though no one knew better than he did the futility of such an attempt. Still he pressed on and might possibly have reached Bazaine but for the unaccountable conduct of that general in neglecting to act on McMahon's despatches and in failing to communicate with him, all of which has formed a great portion of the charges preferred against Bazaine. On endeavoring to reach Metz, McMahon met the Germans at Sedan in overwhelming numbers. Disdaining to retreat or surrender he drew up his small force in order of battle and awaited the enemy's attack. He had not long to wait, for the Germans, fearing that with so diminutive an army he would take the first opportunity to fall back, rushed on him with the force of an avalanche. Then ensued the bloodiest fight of the war. The French would not give way and, imitating the example of their gallant leader, they fought with desperate and even reckless courage, so that it was only on the fall of their heroic commander, wounded, it was supposed mortally, that they acknowledged their defeat and saved themselves from utter annihilation by an army six or seven times their strength.

We now find the Marshal wounded and, for the first time, a prisoner; but though treated with all courtesy and assigned by the Emperor William a residence in the pleasant little village of Pourru-aux-Bois, we can well imagine that the thought of the imbecility, ignorance, and treachery of those who had wrought such woe to his country must have pained more his noble spirit than any bodily ailment or physical suffering. Soon after, the preliminaries of peace between the belligerents were signed, he was released from captivity, and reached Paris in the middle of March, 1872.

What a contrast the metropolis presented to the city he had left in the plenitude of its splendor and gayety only eight months previously! Its emperor a dethroned fugitive, its beautiful empress fled from the very people who had formerly almost worshipped her, and the imperial court scattered in all directions. The Prussians, too, had been at its gates, and their shot had toppled down many a proud turret and spire, and their bombs had razed more than one goodly edifice. And now an enemy more ferocious than the troops of Alaric or Jengis Khan was about to take possession of its palaces and magnificent public buildings and monuments, and to wreak on them, by petroleum and fire, an impotent fury which even the blood of the martyred archbishop and so many of his priests had not satisfied.

Usually, particularly in countries like France, defeated generals, no matter how popular previously, lose caste and sink in public estimation; and to all, of any prominence, who took part in the Franco-Prussian war, this rule was strictly applied, with one exception. That exception was in the case of Marshal McMahon. His skill in manœuvring his troops and his gallantry in fighting so long and so desperately against an enemy much his superior in numbers, his severe wound in the heat of action, and his subsequent dignified conduct while a prisoner, endeared him, if possible, still more to the army, and won him the implicit confidence of all classes. The Provisional Assembly, then at Bordeaux, therefore very wisely appointed him to the command of the army around Paris, and having conferred on him plenary powers, ordered him to rescue the city from the hands of the Communists. He accepted the task with his usual willingness to serve his country, and executed it with his wonted promptness. Nor was it an easy task. Street fighting comes as natural to a Parisian *ouvrier* or *gamin* as his *petit verre* or black bread, and besides, the petrolists had the full control of the guns and ammunition reserved after the surrender of the city to the Germans. It was even suspected that they had many sympathizers in the ranks of the army intended for their reduction.

The Marshal, however, was not to be balked by such opposition, and after several days of hard fighting, driving the Communists from post to post, he entered the city and arrested over ten thousand of the more prominent of the malcontents. In gratitude for his prompt action and signal victory, the delighted people offered him the dictatorship, but he refused it, as he had heretofore refused other offers of political distinction. He contented himself with publishing a proclamation, couched in plain, straightforward language, in which he assured the citizens of the restoration of law and order, and counselled them to exercise moderation, prudence, and forbearance. He then assumed his proper position as commander-in-chief, in which capacity he materially assisted, by his military experience and moral influence, M. Thiers in all his designs, particularly in consolidating and reorganizing the scattered fragments of the army.

While thus employed, the 24th of May, 1873, arrived, a day which will be long remembered in France as the first instance in her history of a change of rulers, and to a certain extent, of the form of government, having been peaceably effected. The Provisional Assembly, which was hurriedly called together to take the place of the defunct empire and treat with the Germans, moved from Bordeaux to Versailles, and virtually voted themselves *en permanence*, with Thiers at their head as a sort of *quasi* president. No actual form of government was authoritatively proclaimed, for no party in the house, republican, monarchist, or imperialist, could command a majority favorable to its particular views. The veteran statesman at the head of the temporary government did indeed, in May, propose the formation of a permanent republic, but after an animated debate he was defeated by a vote of three hundred and sixty-two against three hundred and forty-eight, the Napoleonist, Legitimist, and Orleanist factions having coalesced against him. He therefore resigned his portfolio.

Then arose the question, Who should succeed him and take the helm? None but a man who had the full confidence of the people and the army, whose impartiality was above suspicion, and whose patriotism and integrity had been tried, was fit to be selected at such an eventful crisis and to assume the responsibility of preserving peace and of bringing order out of chaos. That man was McMahon, and when his name was mentioned for President of the Republic in the Assembly it was received with cheers from all sides, and he was forthwith elected. On being formally notified of the high honor conferred on him, with the willingness that ever induced him to set aside his own inclinations when the good of his country demanded the sacrifice, he accepted the responsible trust in the following few, but emphatic words:

MESSIEURS THE REPRESENTATIVES: I obey the will of the Assembly, the depositary of the national sovereignty, in accepting the charge of President of the Republic. It is a heavy responsibility imposed upon my patriotism; but with God's help, the devotion of our army, which will be the army of law, and the support of honest men, we shall continue together the work of the liberation of the territory and the re-establishment of moral order in our country; we shall maintain internal peace and those principles upon which society can repose. In saying this I pledge you my word of honor as an honest man and a soldier.

MARSHAL McMAHON,
Duke of Magenta.

To the prefects of France he addressed, the day following, a brief circular, which read thus:

I have been called, through the confidence of the National Assembly, to the Presidency of the Republic. No immediate change will be made in the existing laws, regulations, and institutions. I rely upon material order, and I count upon you, upon your vigilance, and upon your patriotic assistance. The Ministry will be formed to-day.

The President of the Republic,
MARSHAL McMAHON,
Duke of Magenta.

Once installed in his new office McMahon set to work to complete the labors so auspiciously begun by Thiers, and to heal as quickly as possible the wounds inflicted on the nation during the war. Instalments of the debt to Germany were regularly paid, the country was relieved from the presence of the foreign soldiery, the finances were placed on a more secure footing, industry was promoted, and peace and good order maintained. When the Assembly adjourned, the President promised that during the recess law and justice should rule paramount, and he kept his word faithfully. France was never so satisfied and orderly as in the year of grace A. D. 1873. On the reopening of the Assembly, November 5th in that year, President McMahon addressed to that body a message which read as follows :

When you adjourned for the recess I told you that you could leave Versailles without uneasiness, and that during your absence nothing would occur to disturb the public peace. What I then announced has been realized. In reassembling to-day you find France at peace; the complete liberation of the territory is an accomplished fact; the foreign army has left French soil; and our troops have reëntered the evacuated departments amid the patriotic joy of the population.

The deliverance has been effected without causing trouble at home or awakening distress abroad. Europe is assured of our firm resolution to maintain peace, and without fear sees us again take possession of ourselves. I receive from all powers testimony of their desire to live with us on friendly terms.

At home public order has been firmly maintained. A vigilant administration, confided to the functionaries of different political origin, but all devoted to the cause of order, has strictly applied existing laws. The administration has everywhere acted in the conservative spirit which has always been manifested by the great majority of this Assembly, and from which, as far as I am concerned, I shall never depart so long as you intrust the Government to me.

It is true that material tranquillity has not prevented agitation in the public mind. As the period of your reassembling approached party strife has acquired redoubled intensity. This was to be expected.

Among the matters which you yourselves indicated must claim your attention on resuming your labors, was the examination of the constitutional laws presented by my predecessor.

This necessarily again brings forward the question, always reserved hitherto, of the definitive form of Government. It is not, therefore, surprising that this grave problem should have been raised beforehand by various parties, ardently discussed by each in the sense agreeable to its particular views. I had neither to intervene in this discussion, nor to forestall the decision of your sovereign authority. My Government could do no more than confine the discussion within legal limits, and insure, under any hypothesis, absolute respect for your decision.

Your power is therefore intact, and nothing can impede its exercise. Perhaps, however, you may think that the strong feeling produced by these animated discussions is a proof that, as facts now stand, and with the present state of the public mind, the establishment of any form of government whatever which should indefinitely bind the future, presents serious difficulties. You will, perhaps, find it to be more prudent to maintain in present institutions a character enabling the Government to surround itself, as at present, with all the friends of order without distinction of party.

If you think so, permit him whom you elected to an honor which he did not seek, to tell you frankly his opinion.

To give public peace a sure guarantee, the present Government lacks two essential conditions, of which you cannot longer leave it destitute without danger. It has neither sufficient vitality nor authority. Whatever the holder of power may be, that power can do nothing durable if its right to govern is daily called into question—if it has not before it the guarantee of a sufficiently long existence to spare the country the prospect of incessantly recurring agitation. With a power that might be changed at any moment, it is possible to secure peace to-day, but not safety for the morrow.

Every great undertaking is thus rendered impossible, and industry languishes. France, who only asks to be allowed to enter upon a fresh career, is arrested in her development. In relation with foreign powers her policy cannot acquire that consistent and persevering spirit which alone succeeds in inspiring confidence, and maintains or restores the greatness of a nation.

Stability is wanting in the present Government, and authority also often fails it. It is not sufficiently armed by the laws to discourage the factions, or even to obtain obedience from its own agents. The public press abandons itself with impunity to excesses which would end by corrupting the public mind throughout the country. Municipalities forget that they are organs of law, and leave the central authority without representatives in many parts of the territory.

You will consider these dangers, and will give to society a strong and durable executive power which will be solicitous for its future, and able to defend it with energy.

This message, so terse, comprehensive, and well-timed, was received by every member of the Assembly, if we except a few radicals of the extreme Left, with warm demonstrations of approval, and at the instance of the members of the Right and

Right-centre, moderate monarchists and conservative republicans, a committee was appointed to consider the expediency of prolonging the term of the President, pending the formation of a permanent constitution and the adoption of a definite form of government. Some of McMahon's warmest admirers were for having him retain his high position for life, others for five or ten years, while the extremists were utterly opposed to the whole scheme.

The Marshal himself was of opinion that seven years would be sufficient for his term of office, both as a probable precedent and as affording ample time for him to restore law and order and to extricate France from the confusion and difficulties growing out of the late war. Accordingly, on the 7th of November, 1873, one of the ministers, the Duc de Broglie, read to the Assembly a short message from the President, in which he said that it had been decided as best for the interests of the country to ask of the Assembly the prolongation of the powers of the present Executive for seven years. He deemed it his duty to indicate the guarantees without which it would be improvident for him to accept the task of governing the country. He pointed out the bad effect of a postponement of the beginning of the prolongation until after the constitutional bills were voted. Such a course would diminish his authority, and render it the more uncertain. He expressed the strongest desire for a speedy discussion of the constitutional bills. If his term were prolonged, he would use the powers granted in the defence of conservative ideas, which, he was convinced, were those of the majority of the nation. After the adjournment Ministers De Broglie, Batbie, and Ernoul attended a meeting of the committee on prolongation, and submitted the propositions of the President's message. The committee consented to the term of seven years, but refused to yield on other points.

On the 18th, in the Assembly, General Changarnier presented the motion agreed upon by the Right for the unconditional prolongation of President McMahon's powers. A long and stormy debate followed, but without a division. On the following day the debate was continued on Changarnier's motion for the unconditional prolongation of the President's powers. M. Rouher moved that the question be referred to a *plébiscite*, and advocated his motion in a speech in which he hinted that Providence might in time restore the Bonapartes to power. The excitement over these remarks temporarily suspended the proceedings of the session. A vote upon M. Rouher's motion was finally taken, and it was rejected by a vote of 499 to 88. After an adjournment, the Assembly, as if conscious of the gravity of the task before them, held a night session which lasted till midnight. M. Deperge, a member of the Right, moved an amendment to the report of the committee on prolongation, providing that President McMahon's powers be prolonged seven years, independently of the adoption of the constitutional bills. MM. Laboulaye, Grevy, and others, opposed the amendment, but it was adopted by a majority of 66. A motion was then made on the part of the Right that a Committee of Thirty be appointed to report on the constitutional bills. This was adopted by a majority of 68 votes.

Notwithstanding the lateness of the hour at which this important decision was reached—one of the most important events that has transpired in the political history of the country for many years—the news soon spread throughout Paris, and caused general rejoicing among all classes, always of course leaving out the disorderly and criminal. Men who had anything at stake, either reputation, property, or the productions of their individual skill and manual labor, breathed more freely, and congratulated each other that the Executive of the nation was in the hands of one who was as wise as he was patriotic, and who, while consulting the best interests of France, would sternly repress disorder and fanaticism in whatever form presented. Immediately after the prolongation of his term the President was waited on by the members of his cabinet, who went through the ceremony of tendering their resignation, which he refused to accept, and requested them to retain their portfolios and assist him in the transaction of public affairs as formerly. They consented. On the following day the members of the diplomatic corps waited on his Excellency and presented to him their congratulations.

Thus while the people as a body are delighted with the action of their representatives, all classes, directly or indirectly interested in the rejuvenation of the Republic appear thoroughly satisfied. The republicans are content; the sensible royalists prefer him to any ruler other than one of their many special candidates; the imperialists have confidence in his moderation and prudence, while the army, with which he has always been a great favorite, is overjoyed at the civic honors conferred on the hero of Magenta. Even the Comte de Chambord, "Henry V," who holds himself the rightful heir to the throne, cannot allude to the gallant Marshal but in terms of the highest praise. In a late letter to M. Chesnelong, he refers to McMahon in right royal parlance, as the modern Bayard who has drawn his sword in a hundred battles for France.

Marshal McMahon, though in his sixty-fifth year, is still remarkably robust, and in the complete possession of his physical and mental faculties. In figure he is somewhat above the middle size, meagre, well knit, and erect, though bearing evident marks of the many hardships he has endured and wounds received. His features wear the impress of his nationality; keen gray eyes, short nose, well-formed mouth and chin, and cheek-bones rather angular and prominent. In 1853 he was married to a daughter of the Duc de Castres, by whom he has had children; one of whom, a son, having lately visited Ireland, was very warmly received by the Nationalists there. The Duchess of Magenta is represented as a lady still in the bloom and health of happy middle-age, and remarkable not only for her graces and accomplishments but for her gentle and unceasing charity.

And so we find the President has not only been successful in arms, but equally fortunate in matrimony; and, in entering on his new career as civil ruler of the first nation in Europe there are few in either hemisphere who do not wish that his martial and social good fortune may be but a prelude to a more brilliant career and even more enduring fame. No matter what faults France may have exhibited in the past or what mistakes she has undoubtedly committed in in the present, she is still the best loved nation in the world. We speak not now of Ireland, with whom she has been an ancient ally, nor of the United States, whose friendship for her dates from our birth as a Republic, but of civilized communities generally, who cannot help admiring her soldiers, statesmen, artists, and scholars; who sympathize with her misfortunes, and are made glad in her elevation, and who will doubtless find occasion to feel proud of her new government, when guided by the firm hand of the grandson of an Irish exile, and a devoted French soldier and statesman.

ANDREW JACKSON,

SEVENTH PRESIDENT OF THE UNITED STATES.

OF the large number of Americans distinguished in war or peace, always excepting the great man who has been justly styled *Pater Patriæ*, of which our Republic can be truly proud, one of the foremost in merit and decidedly the most remarkable in origin, character, and originality, was Andrew Jackson, seventh President of the United States. Doubtless we have had greater generals, successful in wider spheres of action, and statesmen more accomplished and profound, but our history presents none who united in himself, in so high a degree, those great and varied, though so dissimilar, qualities which are indispensable for the formation of a conqueror, or for the civil ruler of a great nation.

Born of humble Irish emigrant parents A. D. 1767, in the remote Waxhaw settlements of North Carolina, ere he had passed his boyhood he was left an orphan, without a relative or friend in that wild region, and, as we can well suppose, with little worldly goods. Shortly before his birth, his father, a native Carrickfergus, in the county of Antrim, died, and a few years after, his mother, a woman, it is said, of singular strength of mind and overflowing charity, fell a victim to her devotion to the wants of the fever-stricken patriot prisoners confined in the jails of Charleston, S. C., by the British. His two brothers, older than himself, bravely fought and nobly fell in support of the country of their adoption, for they were not born on this continent. Indeed the whole family seems to have been imbued with an intense spirit of military patriotism, for in 1780, we find young Andrew himself in the ranks of the Continental army, where he remained till victory crowned the long and desperate efforts of the United Colonies.

For some years after, the young orphan cultivated the arts of peace under very adverse circumstances; sometimes engaged in agriculture, and at others in those multifarious pursuits which the sturdy backwoodsman knows so well how to adopt as a means of gaining a livelihood. It was while thus engaged that he laid the foundation of that sturdy, rugged physical constitution which enabled him in after years to perform a vast amount of work without mental or bodily fatigue, and to endure hardships almost incredible with little inconvenience. But he was not content to occupy always this obscure station in life. His ambition took a nobler flight, and, conscious of his own innate powers, he sought to improve his mind as well as to sustain his body. As far as his limited means would allow, and the scant opportunities for mental improvement which that wild district presented, he labored assiduously to acquire at least some knowledge of the language and institutions of his country. This partially accomplished, he commenced the study of law with Judge McKay, and afterwards removed with John McNairy to Tennessee.

Though ill prepared by early training

or previous legal practice, but with an unbending will, ever his chief characteristic, we find him in his new home rapidly advancing to success, gaining so much, step by step, in public confidence, that before the close of the century he occupied a seat on the bench of the Supreme Court, the highest tribunal in the state. "The first time I saw General Jackson," writes a distinguished friend of his, afterwards United States Senator, "was at Nashville, Tennessee, in 1799—he on the bench, a judge of the then Superior Court, and I, a youth of seventeen, back in the crowd. He was then a remarkable man, and had his ascendant over all who approached him, not the effect of his high judicial station, nor of the senatorial rank which he had held and resigned; nor of military exploits, for he had not then been to war; but the effect of personal qualities: cordial and graceful manners, hospitable temper, elevation of mind, undaunted spirit, generosity, and perfect integrity. In charging the jury in the impending case, he committed a slight solecism in language, which grated on my ear, and lodged on my memory, without derogating in the least from the respect which he inspired; and without awakening the slightest suspicion that I was ever to be engaged in smoothing his diction. The first time I spoke with him was some years after, at a (then) frontier town in Tennessee, when he was returning from a Southern visit, which brought him through the towns and camps of some of the Indian tribes. In pulling off his overcoat, I perceived on the white lining of the turning down sleeve, a dark speck, which had life and motion. I brushed it off, and put the heel of my shoe upon it—little thinking that I was ever to brush away from him game of a very different kind. He smiled; and we began a conversation in which he very quickly revealed a leading trait of his character—that of encouraging young men in their laudable pursuits. Getting my name and parentage, and learning my intended profession, he manifested a regard for me, said he had received hospitality at my father's house in

North Carolina, gave me kind invitations to visit him; and expressed a belief that I would do well at the bar—generous words, which had the effect of promoting what they undertook to foretell. Soon after, he had further opportunity to show his generous feelings. I was employed in a criminal case of great magnitude, where the oldest and ablest counsel appeared—Haywood, Grundy, Whiteside—and the trial of which General Jackson attended through concern for the fate of a friend. As junior counsel I had to precede my elders, and did my best; and, it being on the side of his feelings, he found my effort to be better than it was. He complimented me greatly, and from that time our intimacy began."

He had previously been elected Representative in 1796, and Senator in 1797, but he resigned all these positions for the attractions of private life, and retired to his splendid farm of two thousand acres, known as the "Hermitage," about twelve miles from Nashville, where, in the society of his amiable wife and her young relatives, and surrounded by a host of sincere friends, he resolved to pass the remainder of his days far from the bustle and excitement of the political arena. But fate had not so willed it. His repose was soon to be disturbed, and his secluded home to be invaded by the clang of arms, and the voice of his imperilled countrymen. The " Hermitage," was no longer to be a place devoted to quietness and retirement, but to become, in all future times, the shrine at which many a political pilgrim and devotee loved to visit.

In 1812 the tocsin of war was sounded throughout the land from end to end. England and her Indian allies, the barbarians of the old and new world, again menacing the integrity of the Young Republic, were to be once more defied, fought, and defeated, and Jackson, who, at the age of thirteen, had shouldered his gun in the same good cause, was not the man to stand idle while his country was in danger. It was while at the Hermitage, surrounded by his family and friends and in the enjoyment of all that material comfort and domestic harmony could bestow, that the summons reached him; he had been appointed Major-General of the Militia of his State in 1801, and was required to not only lead but raise the quota of Tennessee; and, like a second Cincinnatus, he cheerfully left the plough in the furrow and took up the sword of the warrior. The General Government also commissioned him Brigadier-General, and, two years after, he was promoted to the rank of Major-General of Regulars.

The former choice, in all respects, though effected by a majority of one, was most judicious. He had many friends in the neighborhood, whose confidence in his ability to execute the duties of any office which he assumed was unlimited. He quickly raised a corps of volunteers and commenced operations against the Creek Indians, then in alliance with England, whom, after marches of incredible difficulty and many battles and minor encounters, he completely subdued. Of the former the most important and decisive was that of Tohopeka, fought April, 1814, in which the savages were almost completely annihilated; the last and principal charge on them being led by a gallant Irishman, of whom Jackson says, "the militia of the venerable General Dougherty's brigade acted in the charge with a vivacity and firmness which would have done honor to regulars."

After the declaration of war in 1812, the first series of engagements between the contending forces took place on the Canadian frontier, at the beginning with doubtful success; but eventually the tide of victory turned in favor of the Americans. The same result occurred to the allies of the British, the Creeks, but the national cause in this case was, as we have seen, much more triumphantly sustained. The next move was against our centre. Hâvre-de-Grace, Maryland, having been attacked in May, 1813, and in the August of the following year the battle of Bladensburg was fought, and the city of Washington burned by the English. But their victory was a barren one; and Ross, their general, having been slain, they transferred their scene of operations farther south. On the 22d of December, 1814, General Packenham appeared in the neighborhood of New Orleans, with about fourteen thousand veteran troops, well armed and equipped, thoroughly officered, and supported by a large flotilla and some vessels of war. In the meantime Major-General Jackson, then commanding the seventh division, was ordered to march to the relief of the menaced city; which he did with his usual promptness and celerity, though all the troops he could muster did not number six thousand, some of whom were militia who had served under him in his Indian war, but the majority were raw levies from Tennessee, Kentucky, and Mississippi.

It may well be imagined that a contest between forces so unequally matched could have but one result, and that result far different from the actual one. Of the first encounter, which took place December 23d, the hero himself modestly writes to President Monroe:

"The loss of our gun-boats near the pass of the Rigolets having given the enemy command of Lake Borgne, he was enabled to choose his point of attack. It became, therefore, an object of importance to obstruct the numerous bayous and canals leading from that lake to the highlands on the Mississippi. This important service was committed, in the first instance, to a detachment of the Seventh regiment; afterwards to Col. De Laronde, of the Louisiana militia, and, lastly, to make all sure, to Major-General Villere, commanding the district between the river and the lakes, and who, being a native of the country, was presumed to be best acquainted with all those passes. Unfortunately, however, a picquet which the general had established at the mouth of the Bayou Bienvenue, and which, notwithstanding my orders, had been left unobstructed, was completely surprised, and the enemy penetrated through a canal leading to a farm, about two leagues below the city, and succeeded in cutting off a company of militia stationed there. This intelligence was communicated to me about twelve o'clock of the 23d. My force at this time consisted of parts of the Seventh and Forty-fourth regiments, not exceeding six hundred together, the city militia, a part of General Coffee's brigade of mounted gunmen, and the detached militia from the western division of Tennessee, under the command of Major-General Carroll. These two last corps were stationed four miles above the city. Apprehending a double attack by the way of Chief-Menteur, I left General Carroll's force and the militia of the city posted on the Gentilly road; and at five o'clock P. M. marched to meet the enemy, whom I was resolved to attack in his first position, with Major Hinds's dragoons, General Coffee's brigade, parts of the Seventh and Forty-fourth regiments, the uniformed companies of militia, under the command of Major Planche, two hundred men of color, chiefly from St. Domingo, raised by Colonel Savary, and under the command of Major Dagwin, and a detachment of artillery under the direction of Colonel M'Rhea, with two six-pounders, under the command of Lieutenant Spotts; not exceeding, in all, fifteen hundred. I arrived near the enemy's encampment about seven, and immediately made my dispositions for the attack. His forces, amounting at that time on land to about three thousand, extended half a mile on that river, and in the rear nearly to the wood. General Coffee was ordered to turn their right, while, with the residue of the force, I attacked his strongest position on the left, near the river. Commodore Patterson, having dropped down the river in the schooner Caroline, was directed to open a fire upon their camp, which he executed at about half-past seven. This being a signal of attack, General Coffee's men, with their usual impetuosity, rushed on the enemy's right, and entered their camp, while our right advanced with equal ardor. There can be but little doubt that we should have succeeded on that occasion, with our inferior force, in destroying or capturing the enemy, had not a thick fog, which arose about eight o'clock, occasioned some confusion among the different corps. Fearing the consequence, under this circumstance, of the further prosecution of a night attack, with troops then acting together for the first time, I contented myself with lying on the field that night; and at four in the morning assumed a stronger position, about two miles nearer the city. At this position I remained encamped, waiting the arrival of the Kentucky militia and other reinforcements. As the safety of the city will depend on the fate of this army, it must not be incautiously exposed.

"In this affair the whole corps under my command deserve the greatest credit. The best compliment I can pay to General Coffee and his brigade is, to say they have behaved as they have always done while under my command. The Seventh, led by Major Pierre, and Forty-fourth, commanded by Colonel Ross, distinguished themselves. The battalion of city militia, commanded by Major Planche, realized my anticipations, and behaved like veterans. Savary's volunteers manifested great bravery; and the company of city riflemen, having penetrated into the midst of the enemy's camp, were surrounded, and fought their way out with the greatest heroism, bringing with them a number of prisoners. The two field-pieces were well served by the officers commanding them.

"All my officers in the line did their duty, and I have every reason to be satisfied with the whole of my field and staff. Colonels Butler and Platt, and Major Chotard, by their intrepidity, saved the artillery. Colonel Haynes was everywhere that duty or danger called. I was deprived of the services of one of my aids, Captain Butler, whom I was obliged to station, to his great regret, in town. Captain Reid, my other aid, and Messrs. Livingston, Duplissis, and Davezac, who had volunteered their services, faced danger wherever it was to be met, and carried my orders with the utmost promptitude.

"We made one major, two subalterns, and sixty-three privates, prisoners; and the enemy's loss, in killed and wounded, must have been at least ———. My own loss I have not as yet been able to ascertain with exactness, but suppose it to amount to one hundred in killed, wounded, and missing. Among the former, I have to lament the loss of Colonel Lauderdale, of General Coffee's brigade, who fell while bravely fighting. Cols. Dyer and Gibson, of the same corps, were wounded, and Major Kavenaugh taken prisoner.

"Colonel De Laronde, Major Villere, of the Louisiana militia, Major Latour of Engineers, having no command, volunteered their services, as did Drs. Kerr and Hood, and were of great assistance to me."

Of the great battle, that of the 8th of January, 1815, the following graphic, yet glowing description, from the pen of a contemporary writer thoroughly master of his subject will be found of even greater interest:

"On the seventh, a general movement and bustle in the British camp indicated that the contemplated attack was about to be made. Everything in the American encampment was ready for action, when, at daybreak, on the morning of the memorable eighth, a shower of rockets from the enemy gave the signal of battle. A detachment of the enemy, under Colonel Thornton, proceeded to attack the works on the right bank of the river, while General Pakenham, with his whole force, exceeding twelve thousand men, moved in two divisions under Generals Gibbs and Kean, and a reserve under General Lambert. Both divisions were supplied with scaling-ladders and fascines, and General Gibbs had directions to make the principal attack. Nothing could exceed the imposing grandeur of the scene. The whole British force advanced with much deliberation, in solid columns, over the even surface of the plain in front of the American intrenchments, bearing with them, in addition to their arms, their fascines and ladders for storming the American works. All was hushed in awful stillness throughout the American lines; each soldier grasped his arms with a fixedness of purpose, which told his firm resolve to 'do or die;' till the enemy approached within reach of the batteries, which opened upon them an incessant and destructive tide of death. They continued, however, to advance with the greatest firmness, closing up their lines as they were opened by the fire of the Americans, till they approached within reach of the musketry and rifles; these, in addition to the artillery, produced the most terrible havoc in their ranks, and threw them into the greatest confusion. Twice were they driven back with immense slaughter, and twice they formed again and renewed the assault. But the fire of the Americans was tremendous; it was unparalleled in the annals of deadly doing; it was one continued blaze of destruction, before which men could not stand and live. Every discharge swept away the British columns like an inundation—they could not withstand it, but fled in consternation and dismay. Vigorous were the attempts of their officers to rally them; General Pakenham, in the attempt, received a shot, and fell upon the field. Generals Gibbs and Kean succeeded, and attempted again to push on their columns to the attack, but a still more dreadful fatality met them from the thunders of the American batteries. A third unavailing attempt was made to rally their troops by their officers, but the same destruction met them. The gallantry of the British officers, on this desperate day, was deserving of a worthier cause and better fate. General Gibbs fell mortally, and General Kean desperately wounded, and were borne from the field of action. The discomfiture of the enemy was now complete; a few only of the platoons reached the ditch, there to meet more certain death. The remainder fled from the field with the greatest precipitancy, and no further efforts were made to rally them. The intervening plain between the American and British fortifications was covered with the dead; taking into view the length of time and the numbers engaged, the annals of bloody strife, it is believed, furnish no parallel to the dreadful carnage of this battle. Two thousand, at the lowest estimate, fell, besides a considerable number wounded.

The loss of the Americans did not exceed seven killed and six wounded. General Lambert was the only superior officer left on the field; being unable to check the flight of the British columns, he retreated to his encampment."

We cannot better close an account of this, Jackson's, grandest military achievement, than by quoting the terse reply of Senator Thomas Benton to Monsieur de Tocqueville, *à propos* of the victory and the victor: "It was no ordinary achievement. It was a victory of 4,600 citizens just called from their homes, without knowledge of scientific war, under a leader as little schooled as themselves in that particular, without other advantages than a slight field-work (a ditch and a bank of earth) hastily thrown up— over double their numbers of British veterans, survivors of the wars of the French Revolution, victors in the Peninsula and at Toulouse, under trained generals of the Wellington school, and with a disparity of loss never before witnessed. On one side 700 killed (including the first, second, and third generals); 1,400 wounded; 500

taken prisoners. On the other, six privates killed, and seven wounded; and the total repulse of an invading army which instantly fled to its 'wooden walls,' and never again placed a hostile foot on American soil. Such an achievement is not ordinary, much less 'very' ordinary. Does Monsieur de Tocqueville judge the importance of victories by the numbers engaged, and the quantity of blood shed, or by their consequences? If the former, the cannonade on the heights of Valmy (which was not a battle, nor even a combat, but a distant cannon firing in which few were hurt), must seem to him a very insignificant affair. Yet it did what the marvellous victories of Champaubert, Montmirail, Château-Thierry, Vauchamps, and Montereau could not do—turned back the invader, and saved the soil of France from the iron hoof of the conqueror's horse! and was commemorated twelve years afterwards by the great emperor in a ducal title bestowed upon one of its generals. The victory at New Orleans did what the cannonade at Valmy did—drove back the invader! and also what it did not do—destroyed the one fourth part of his force. And, therefore, it is not to be disparaged, and will not be, by any one who judges victories by their consequences, instead of by the numbers engaged. And so the victory at New Orleans will remain in history as one of the great achievements of the world, in spite of the low opinion which the writer on American democracy entertains of it."

In those days of slow communication the news of this great victory only reached Washington on the 4th of February; and, as might be expected, caused intense and universal joy, not only in the national capital but throughout the entire country. Congress unanimously passed a vote of thanks to the victor and his subordinates, and ordered a gold medal to be struck and presented to the general, commemorative of the event. The populace, also, independent of all party affiliations, expressed in the most enthusiastic terms their admiration for the hero of New Orleans and his gallant little army. The press of the day, such as it was, taxed its utmost energies to laud his bravery and skill; patriotic gatherings passed glowing resolutions of commendation, and toasts were everywhere drank in his honor.

This jubilant state of public feeling was still more heightened by the arrival, a few days after, of a ship at New York, with news of the ratification of the treaty of Ghent, by which peace between the United States and England was again restored, and the demands of the former country substantially conceded. It is worthy of notice that this treaty was signed in December, 1814; so that in fact the respective nations of Jackson and Packenham, on the day of the battle of New Orleans, were no longer enemies; but the vessel employed to bring the intelligence to our shores was delayed by storms and adverse winds and only succeeded in making her port on the 11th of February, 1815.

Jackson remained in New Orleans three months after the battle. Like a prudent and humane commander his first care was for his wounded and almost naked troops, and in this he was most zealously and efficiently assisted by the citizens. Private houses were thrown open for the reception of the sufferers; blankets, mattresses, and clothing of every description were cheerfully and voluntarily supplied; and all classes and sexes vied, one with the other, in their attention to the brave men who had defended their homes and liberties. When the enemy had disappeared and all danger of his return had vanished, the troops were removed from the city to a more salubrious position.

It is needless to say that at that time the population of New Orleans, mostly French or of French origin, were, almost without exception, Catholic, and their devotion to the cause of the United States was no doubt heightened by their national and religious antipathy to England; then, as ever, the most bitter persecutor of the Church. An incident which occurred on the eve of the battle of the 8th well illustrates this feeling. It was related many years after, at a celebration meeting, by Mr. Livingston, a United

States senator, who was a participant in the action. He said:

"In the city of New Orleans is a convent in which a number of respectable ladies have dedicated their lives to the practice of piety, to the education of poor children of their own sex, and to works of charity. This pious sisterhood were awakened from their rest, or disturbed in their holy vigils, before the dawn of the 8th of January, by the roar of cannon and volleys of musketry. The calendar which pointed out the prayers of the day was hastily opened, and indicated the auspicious name of St. Victoria. They hailed the omen, and prostrate on the pavement which 'holy knees had worn,' implored the God of Battles to nerve the arm of their protectors and turn the tide of combat against the invaders of their country. Their prayers were heard. And, while they daily offer up their thanks to the Power to whose aid they ascribe their deliverance, they have not been unmindful of him who was chosen as the instrument to effect it."

Though by no means a religious man, much less a zealot, Jackson could not but ascribe his unexpected triumph to an agency higher than any mere human means. Accordingly, as soon as his wounded were attended to and his famished men fed and clothed, he addressed to the Abbé Dubourg a request, couched in most appropriate and Christian terms, that he would cause a *Te Deum* to be sung in the cathedral, in thanksgiving for the victory. The favor was cheerfully granted, and on the 23d of January the citizens of New Orleans witnessed a spectacle such as had never been seen in its streets before or subsequently. The avenue to the cathedral was lined with spectators in holiday garb, the houses on either side being decorated with garlands and flags, while at intervals, floral arches of triumph were thrown across from house to house. Up this street came Jackson in, full uniform, attended by his staff and many of his officers, and escorted by the most prominent citizens. At the vestibule of the church he was met by the venerable Abbé, in full canonicals, and welcomed in a brief, but highly eulogistic and dignified address. The General replied in a similar strain and the whole party entered the cathedral, when the noblest hymn of the Catholic Church was chanted, its notes of gratitude and exaltation finding a responsive echo in thousands of grateful hearts.

Jackson departed for his home, in April, having previously been the recipient of every honor and favor that an enthusiastic and warm-hearted people could bestow. With the ladies in particular he seems to have been an especial favorite, and they were never tired of showing their appreciation of the services he had rendered them, and to Mrs. Jackson, who came down to visit her husband, they were particularly hospitable and attentive. Their delicacy and kindness in this respect were more grateful to the General than any compliment they could have paid himself.

After four months' rest at the Hermitage, Jackson proceeded to Washington City by easy stages; for his health, which had been exceedingly precarious at the breaking out of the war, was even more enfeebled by exposure and privation in the field. Every town, village, and hamlet through which he passed on his route received him with the greatest enthusiasm, and the few large cities which at that time lay between Nashville and the capital serenaded and fêted him to such a degree that he was glad to escape so oppressive but well-meant attentions.

On arriving at his destination he was very cordially received by the Executive, and confirmed in his rank of Major-General, with the command of the south-west. The members of both branches of Congress, also, were unremitting in their politeness, some from a sense, no doubt, of his popularity and growing influence in public affairs, and others from higher motives. He did not, however, remain long in Washington, for we find him at his headquarters in Nashville, in October of the following year, having turned aside from his homeward journey to visit the Indian country and some of the more important posts of his command. In March, 1817, on the accession of Mr. Monroe to the presidency, he was offered the position of Secretary of War, but declined it, from a conviction that he was more useful to the country in his present capacity. He foresaw that an Indian war was imminent, and was resolved to command in it.

His foresight, as usual, was correct. In this very year the Seminoles of Florida, a very powerful and warlike tribe, instigated by a Scotch trader named Arbuthnot, an English ex-midshipman named Ambrister, and several other adventurers from the neighboring Bahamas, commenced depredations on the settlers of the frontiers of Georgia, during which a great many white men were mercilessly slaughtered, and those taken captive put to death with inhuman tortures. General Gaines at first endeavored to check the savages, and to some extent succeeded, but Jackson was convinced that no half measures would ever succeed against so wily and implacable an enemy. The foe must not only be beaten out of Georgia, but pursued and destroyed in Florida, before peace could be permanently restored.

Florida at that time was a colony of Spain, a country at peace with ours, and an armed invasion of its soil, under ordinary circumstances, would of course be a breach of the law of nations and a violation of our treaty stipulations. But the circumstances were not ordinary. A part of it around Negro Point was held by an armed force of runaway negroes; and another, Pensacola, by Scotch and English filibusters; while the Seminoles, supplied by the latter with arms and ammunition, invaded at pleasure the Georgian frontiers and, when beaten back, took refuge under the guns of one or other fort. The Spanish Captain-General was unable or unwilling to keep those lawless banditti in order, so it became the duty of our Government, in protecting the lives and property of its citizens, to take the matter into its own hands.

General Jackson saw the necessity of such a decisive step, but, unwilling to involve the country in a foreign dispute, proposed "to take the responsibility" on himself. He therefore wrote a confidential letter to the President, in which the following significant paragraphs occur:

"The Executive Government have ordered, and, as I conceive, very properly, Amelia Island to be taken possession of. This order ought to be carried into execution at all hazards, and simultaneously the whole of East Florida seized and held as an indemnity for the outrages of Spain upon the property of our citizens. This done, it puts all opposition down, secures our citizens a complete indemnity, and saves us from a war with Great Britain, or some of the Continental powers, combined with Spain. This can be done without implicating the government. Let it be signified to me through any channel (say Mr. J. Rhea), that the possession of the Floridas would be desirable to the United States, and in sixty days it will be accomplished.

"The order being given for the possession of Amelia Island, it ought to be executed, or our enemies, internal and external, will use it to the disadvantage of the government. If our troops enter the territory of Spain in pursuit of our Indian enemy, all opposition that they meet with must be put down, or we will be involved in danger and disgrace."

"In accordance with the advice of Mr. Calhoun," says Jackson himself, in his "Exposition," "and availing himself of the suggestion contained in the letter, Mr. Monroe sent for Mr. John Rhea (then a member of Congress), showed him the confidential letter, and requested him to answer it. In conformity with this request Mr. Rhea did answer the letter, and informed General Jackson that the President had shown him the confidential letter, and requested him to state that he approved of its suggestions. This answer was received by the General on the second night he remained at Big Creek, which is four miles in advance of Hartford, Georgia, and before his arrival at Fort Scott, to take command of the troops in that quarter."

The Secretary of War, Calhoun, also sent orders directly to General Jackson "to adopt the necessary measures to put an end to the conflict without regard to territorial lines or Spanish forts." And yet for this very invasion of Florida, Jackson was not only severely blamed, but the Secretary, who had countenanced the measure, was the first, in cabinet council, to advise his trial by court-martial; and, this afterwards becoming known, led to the rupture between them in 1831, when President and Vice-President. The General's statement of his position at that time is terse and to the point. He writes:

"Having received further details of my preparations, not only to terminate the Seminole war, but, as the President and his Secretary well knew, *to occupy Florida also*, Mr. Calhoun on the 6th February writes as follows:

"'I have the honor to acknowledge the receipt of your letter of the 20th ult., and to acquaint you with the entire approbation of the President of all the measures you have adopted to terminate the rupture with the Indians.'

"On the 13th of May following, with a full knowledge that I intended, if a favorable occasion presented itself, to occupy Florida, and that the design had the approbation of the President, Mr. Calhoun wrote to Governor Bibb, of Alabama, the letter already alluded to, concluding as follows:

"'General Jackson is vested with full powers to conduct the war in the manner he may deem best.'

"On the 25th of March, 1818, I informed Mr. Calhoun that I intended to occupy St. Mark's, and on the 8th of April I informed him that it was done.

"Not a whisper of disapprobation or of doubt reached me from the government.

"On the 5th May I wrote to Mr. Calhoun that I was about to move upon Pensacola with a view of occupying that place.

"Again, no reply was ever given disapproving or discountenancing this movement.

"On the 2d of June I informed Mr. Calhoun that I had on the 24th May entered Pensacola, and on the 28th had received the surrender of the Barrancas.

"Again no reply was given to this letter, expressing any disapproval of these acts.

"In fine, from the receipt of the President's reply to my confidential letter of 6th January, 1818, through Mr. Rhea, until the receipt of the President's private letter, dated 19th July, 1818, I received no instructions or intimation from the government, public or private, that my operations in Florida were other than such as the President and Secretary of War expected and approved. I had not a doubt that I had acted in every respect in strict accordance with their views, and that without publicly avowing that they had authorized my measures, they were ready at all times and under all circumstances to sustain me; and that as there were sound reasons and justifiable cause for taking possession of Florida, they would, in pursuance of their private understanding with me, retain it as indemnity for the spoliations committed by Spanish subjects on our citizens, and as security for the peace of our Southern frontier.

Acting under instructions, General Jackson left Nashville in January, 1818, and reached the seat of operations in March following. His troops consisted of eight hundred regulars, one thousand militia, and some Tennessee volunteers, whom he had raised on his own responsibility. His movements were rapid. On April 4th he took St. Mark's and shortly after Pensacola, and while in the former place Arbuthnot and Ambrister, the evil genii of the Seminoles, having been captured, were court-martialled and, in accordance with the findings of the court, were executed. Jackson returned to Fort Gadsden in May, but, obtaining information that Pensacola had again become a *refugium peccatorum*, he marched again on that place, occupied it permanently with a detachment of his troops, shortly after took possession of St. Carlos de Barrancas, and thus ended the war. Two years subsequently Florida became a part of the United States.

While General Jackson was receiving on his return the hearty greetings of his fellow-citizens of Tennessee, Congress was deliberating as to the advisability of censuring, not only his late conduct, but hints were even thrown out that he ought to be subjected to disgrace and punishment. The House had the good sense to reject such absurd propositions by a vote of ninety to fifty-four; but the Senate held the matter under advisement for a long time, and finally did nothing.

Having been appointed governor of the newly acquired territory by President Monroe, Major-General Jackson, on the 31st of May, 1821, resigned his commission in the army. Here his military record ceases, and here also, at the advanced age of fifty-four, his career as a statesman begins.

In the spring of 1821, he proceeded to Florida to discharge his new civic duties, but finding them so onerous, and his powers so limited, he soon resigned the office and once more returned to the beloved

Hermitage, now rebuilt and arranged more in accordance with advancing taste and his altered fortunes. In recognition of his great services, the Legislature, in 1823, elected him U. S. Senator for the term of six years, but though he took his seat in the Senate, and voted on some important questions, always on the democratic side, he remained in Washington during but two sessions, and then resigned. The atmosphere of the national capital still seemed distasteful to him.

In 1824, there was a presidential election. There were four candidates, the friends of each of whom were anxious to see their candidate the successor of Mr. Monroe; viz., General Jackson, John Q. Adams, Wm. H. Crawford, and Henry Clay. There was, however, no choice in the electoral college, and the election was consequently thrown into the House of Representatives. According to the Constitution the names of the three highest could only be presented, and these were: Jackson 99, Adams 84, and Crawford 41; Mr. Clay having received only

37 electoral votes. The majority of the house declared for Adams, influenced, it was alleged, by Clay and his supporters, from unworthy motives. That this was a calumny on that illustrious man there can now be little doubt, if we take for granted the statement of his political opponent, Senator Benton. He says, in his "Thirty Years' View":

"It came within my knowledge (for I was then intimate with Mr. Clay), long before the election, and probably before Mr. Adams knew it himself, that Mr. Clay intended to support him against General Jackson; and for the reasons afterward averred in his public speeches. I made this known when occasions required me to speak of it, and in the presence of the friends of the impugned parties. It went into the newspapers upon the information of these friends, and Mr. Clay made me acknowledgments for it in a letter, of which this is the exact copy:

"I have received a paper published on the 20th ultimo, at Lemington, in Virginia, in which is contained an article stating that you had, to a gentleman of that place, expressed your disbelief of a charge injurious to me, touching the late presidential election, and that I had communicated to you unequivocally, before the 15th of December, 1824, my determination to vote for Mr. Adams and not for General Jackson. Presuming that the publication was with your authority, I cannot deny the expression of proper acknowledgments for the sense of justice which has prompted you to render this voluntary and faithful testimony."

If there had been any corrupt dealing between Adams and Clay to defeat Jackson he was fully avenged during the next presidential contest, when he was elected over his former successful rival by a vote of one hundred and seventy-eight to eighty-three; John C. Calhoun being also chosen Vice-President by a little less majority. He was accordingly inaugurated on the 4th of March in the year following, the oath of office being administered by Chief-Justice Marshall. His cabinet was composed of Martin Van Buren (N. Y.), Secretary of State; Samuel D. Ingham (Penn.), of the Treasury; John H. Eaton (Tenn.), at War; John Branch (N. C.), of the Navy; John M. Berrien (Ga.), Attorney-General; Wm. T. Barry (Ky.), Postmaster-General. The Senate—which at this time consisted of forty-eight members, presented on its rolls some of the ablest men of the country, such as Webster, Benton, Grundy, Livingston, Foot, and Tyler—were opposed to the political views of the new President, in the proportion of about three to two, while the popular branch of Congress was largely in his favor.

His first annual message, delivered December 8th, though perhaps not altogether his own composition, at all events not uninspired by his political advisers, was yet replete with his spirit, and ominous of the important questions which were destined to agitate the country for many years after their utterance. He took what has been called strong "democratic ground," and for the first time enunciated from the presidential chair those peculiar views which have since been entertained by one of the two great parties that divide the country. In this respect Jackson may well be styled the Father of the Democratic party. He also recommended the reduction of the army and navy, and broke ground against the United States Bank; a fortress which, after many desperate assaults, he finally succeeded in capturing. His first attack on that institution was couched in the following significant terms:

"The charter of the Bank of the United States expires in 1836, and its stockholders will most probably apply for a renewal of their privileges. In order to avoid the evils resulting from precipitancy in a measure involving such important principles, and such deep pecuniary interests, I feel that I cannot, in justice to the parties interested, too soon present it to the deliberate consideration the legislature and the people. Both the constitutionality and the expediency of the law creating this bank, are well questioned by a large portion of our fellow-citizens; and it must be admitted by all, that it has failed in the great end of establishing a uniform and sound currency."

The first year of Jackson's term was not marked by any important event, foreign or domestic, except the removal of some prominent office-holders and the appointment of persons more in accord with his political views, to fill their places. And here let it be remarked that the popular notion that he was the originator of the policy of "to the victors belong the spoils" is utterly without foundation. His removals for political reasons, in point of fact, were less numerous than those of many of his predecessors, and far less than these of every one who succeeded him in the presidency.

His second year was distinguished by a treaty negotiation with Great Britain, by which unobstructed trade with her West India colonies, lost by the Revolution, was restored. Free commercial intercourse with those islands was very desirable; and attempts had been made by every president, from Washington down, to obtain it by negotiation, but had failed, till our minister,

Mr. Van Buren, acting under the direction of the President, succeeded. An act of Congress was passed May 29th, 1830, to open the ports of the United States to vessels of Great Britain, on condition of her removing all restraints on the West India traffic, which, with the President's proclamation of October 5th, giving it effect, afforded general satisfaction to the mercantile community. "The loss of this trade," says Mr. Benton, "was a great injury to the United States (besides the insult), and was attended by circumstances which gave it the air of punishment for something that was past. It was a rebuff in the face of Europe; for, while the United States were sternly and unceremoniously cut off from the benefit of the act of 1825, for omission to accept it within the year, yet other powers in the same predicament (France, Spain, and Russia) were permitted to accept after the year; and the "irritated feelings" manifested by Mr. Huskisson indicated a resentment which was finding its gratification. We were ill-treated, and felt it. The people felt it. It was an ugly case to manage, or to endure; and in this period of its worst aspect General Jackson was elected President."

In 1831, the rupture between the President and Mr. Calhoun, alluded to above, took place, and was productive, at the time, of much personal feeling as well as fraught with lasting consequences injurious alike to their party and the country. It was commenced by the latter, who, in March of that year, accused Mr. Van Buren of having endeavored to create dissensions between the two highest executive officers of the government. The whole subject arose out of the invasion of Florida and the conduct of Mr. Calhoun when Secretary at War at that time. We have seen that he had ordered General Jackson to prosecute and end the war as he saw fit; but afterwards, it seems, in secret cabinet meeting, condemned his method and suggested his punishment. This, of course, was unknown for many years to Jackson, who looked on Calhoun as his best and most respected friend, and the latter certainly gave him every reason to think so. It was only about two years after their election on the same ticket that Jackson discovered the base deception that had been practised on him, and, with that abhorrence of duplicity which characterized him, he discontinued all personal intercourse with the vice-president. Henceforward Calhoun, in and out of Congress, was his most bitter enemy. Van Buren, though an innocent party to the quarrel, nevertheless felt called on to resign his position as Secretary of State, and was shortly after appointed minister to England. This led necessarily to the breaking up of the cabinet and the formation of a new one, whose views were more in harmony with the chief executive. The new Secretaries were: Edward Livingston (La.), of State; Louis McLane (Del.), of the Treasury; Louis Cass (Mich.), at War; Levi Woodbury (N. H.), of the Navy; Amos Kendall (Ky.), Postmaster-General; Roger Brooke Taney (Md.), Attorney-General.

The twenty-second Congress commenced its first session on the 5th of December,

1831, and was protracted far into the middle of the following summer, during which questions of the most vital importance, particularly on finance, were discussed in both houses, to which the message gave the key-note. The condition and existence of the Bank of the United States was specially alluded to thus: "Entertaining the opinions heretofore expressed in relation to the Bank of the United States, as at present organized, I felt it my duty, in my former messages, frankly to disclose them, in order that the attention of the legislature and the people should be seasonably directed to that important subject, and that it might be considered and finally disposed of in a manner best calculated to promote the ends of the constitution, and subserve the public interests. Having thus conscientiously discharged a constitutional duty, I deem it proper, on this occasion, without a more particular reference to the views of the subject then expressed, to leave it, for the present, to the investigation of an enlightened people and their representatives."

This institution was chartered in 1816, soon after the close of the war, and was intended to relieve the money pressure and disarranged financial condition of the country, consequent on that strruggle. It had, however, it was claimed by its opponents, failed to effect the desired objects, and instead of proving a blessing to the manufacturing, commercial, and agricultural interests of the country, it grew into an oppressive monopoly, controlling, by its six branches in various States, the smaller and weaker moneyed concerns. It was also the depository of the government funds, and, it was alleged against it, used them for the purpose of private speculation. To its friends in Congress, the press, and elsewhere, it had been liberal of discounts and loans, and not over-particular as to the security, and this, with its large capital and extensive ramifications, made it a real power in the land; which was thought by many, and not without reason, to be inimical to the spirit of Republican institutions. From the first, President Jackson resolved, if not to destroy it, at least to curtail its immense proportions.

The charter of the bank was to expire by limitation in 1836, but on the 9th of January, 1832, Mr. Dallas presented a memorial from the president and directors, asking for its renewal in advance. This was the signal for the combat between its friends and enemies. The debates which arose on this subject in the House and Senate were long, acrimonious, and replete with a full knowledge of the subject in all its bearings. In the Senate Mr. Webster was the chief advocate of the bank, and Mr. Benton the leading opponent of the renewal of its charter. The prayer of the memorial, however, was granted by that body by a vote of twenty-eight yeas to twenty nays, and the bill was sent to the House. Here the struggle was even more obstinate, and, if possible, more hotly and persistently carried on, for its success or failure was looked upon as a party defeat or triumph. It was at length, however, carried in the affirmative by a majority of twenty-two out of an entire vote of one hundred and ninety. The bill was then, on the 4th of July, 1832, sent to the President for his signature. It was now Jackson's turn to act, and he did so with a promptness and decision all his own. Though on the eve of another presidential election, and knowing full well that to provoke the hostility of the monster moneyed power was to raise up against himself and his party a most active, unscrupulous, and indefatigable enemy, he hesitated not a moment in his course. Six days after the passage of the bill, he returned it, with his *Veto.* The reasons for this decisive step, as given by the President, were numerous and cogent. Some were of a local or temporary nature, and therefore not worth reproduction at this day; but the following, as they apply to all times, are as applicable to us as to our ancestors.

"Every monopoly, and all exclusive privileges, are granted at the expense of the public, which ought to receive a fair equivalent. The many millions which this act proposes to bestow on the stockholders of the existing bank, must come, directly or indirectly, out of the earnings of the American people. It is due to them, therefore, if their government sell monopolies and exclusive privileges, that they should at least exact for them as much as they are worth in open market. The value of the monopoly in this case may be correctly ascertained. The twenty-eight millions of stock would probably be at an advance of fifty per cent., and command, in market, at least forty-two millions of dollars, subject to the payment of the present loans. The present value of the monopoly, therefore, is seventeen millions of dollars, and this the act proposes to sell for three millions, payable in fifteen annual instalments of $200,000 each.

"It is not conceivable how the present stockholders can have any claim to the special favor of the government. The present corporation has enjoyed its monopoly during the period stipulated in the original contract. If we must have such a corporation, why should not the government sell out the whole stock, and thus secure to the people the full market value of the privileges granted? Why should not Congress create and sell the twenty-eight millions of stock, incorporating the purchasers with all the powers and privileges secured in this act, and putting the premium upon the sales into the treasury? . . . .

"But this proposition, although made by men whose aggregate wealth is believed to be equal to all the private stock in the existing bank, has been set aside, and the bounty of our government is proposed to be again bestowed on the few who have been fortunate enough to secure the stock, and at this moment wield the power of the existing institution. I cannot perceive the justice or policy of this course. If our government must sell monopolies, it would seem to be its duty to take nothing less than their full value; and if gratuities must be made once in fifteen or twenty years, let them not be bestowed on the subjects of a foreign government, nor upon a designated or favored class of men in our own country. It is but justice and good policy, as far as the nature of the case will admit, to confine our favors to our own fellow-citizens, and let each in his turn enjoy an opportunity to profit by our bounty. In the bearings of the act before me upon these points, I find ample reason why it should not become a law."

The veto was sustained, the bank and its defenders were defeated, and the press, throughout the country hostile to the President, commenced a campaign of abuse, ridicule, misrepresentation, and calumny against its author which lasted not only during his second term but long after the organization sought to be perpetuated, had ceased to exist.

Another question of great importance upon which President Jackson held decided opinions was a Protective Tariff. Of course he was against it, and his views were ably elucidated in the Senate by such men as Benton and Hayne of South Carolina, while they were opposed by Webster, Clay, and Dallas. In 1832, a debate occurred on this yet unsettled question, in which Clay took the leading part, and in the course of a long and very profound speech summed up the policy of the protectionist party of that day in the following terms:

"1. That the policy which we have been considering ought to continue to be regarded as the genuine American system.

"2. That the free trade system, which is proposed as its substitute, ought really to be considered as the British colonial system.

"3. That the American system is beneficial to all parts of the Union, and absolutely necessary to much the larger portion.

"4. That the price of the great staple of cotton, and of all our chief productions of agriculture, has been sustained and upheld, and a decline averted, by the protective system.

"5. That, if the foreign demand for cotton has been at all diminished by the operation of that system, the diminution has been more than compensated in the additional demand created at home.

"6. That the constant tendency of the

system, by creating competition among ourselves, and between American and European industry, reciprocally acting upon each other, is to reduce prices of manufactured objects.

"7. That, in point of fact, objects within the scope of the policy of protection have greatly fallen in price.

"8. That if, in a season of peace, these benefits are experienced, in a season of war, when the foreign supply might be cut off, they would be much more extensively felt.

"9. And, finally, that the substitution of the British colonial system for the American system, without benefiting any section of the Union, by subjecting us to a foreign legislation, regulated by foreign interests, would lead to the prostration of our manufactures, general impoverishment, and ultimate ruin."

Another presidential election took place in November, 1832. The candidates of the Democracy were Andrew Jackson and Martin Van Buren; of the Whig party Henry Clay and John Sergeant. The former received each two hundred and thirty-nine votes, to forty-nine for their opponents. Jackson's policy was therefore triumphant. The country was overwhelming democratic, and he entered on his second term with renewed vigor and vastly increased popular support. Still the Senate, which from its construction is slower to feel the effects of a change in public opinion than any other branch of the government, was against him, while the House was even more strongly in his favor. Under the circumstances, however, this division of opinion was a source of security to the country; checking as it did, the impetuosity or heedlessness of the executive and coördinate branch of the legislative authority, and affords another proof, if any additional were wanting, of the wisdom and forethought of the founders of the Republic.

In the annual message immediately after his reëlection, among other things, the President, with a modest but just pride, spoke of his past administration thus:

"I cannot too cordially congratulate Congress and my fellow-citizens on the near approach of that memorable and happy event, the extinction of the public debt of this great and free nation. Faithful to the wise and patriotic policy marked out by the legislation of the country for this object, the present administration has devoted to it all the means which a flourishing commerce has supplied, and a prudent economy preserved, for the public treasury. Within the four years for which the people have confided the executive power to my charge, fifty-eight millions of dollars will have been applied to the payment of the public debt. That this has been accomplished without stinting the expenditures for all other proper objects, will be seen by referring to the liberal provision made, during the same period, for the support and increase of our means of maritime and military defence, for internal improvements of a national character, for the removal and preservation of the Indians, and, lastly, for the gallant veterans of the Revolution."

On the subject of protection he was of opinion that "those who take an enlarged view of the condition of our country, must be satisfied that the policy of protection must be ultimately limited to those articles of domestic manufacture which are indispensable to our safety in time of war." Referring to the position of the public lands he declared that the true policy was, that they should cease, as soon as practicable, to be a source of revenue, but that they should be sold to actual settlers in limited quantities, at a price only sufficient to reimburse the United States for the cost of surveys, Indian compacts, etc. He also expressed himself in favor of the speedy removal of the Indians from Georgia, and their settlement beyond the Mississippi. But the message contained two passages of far greater import than any of the preceding; one relating to the United States Bank and the other to the new political heresy of States Rights or nullification.

His veto of the act re-chartering the bank, as we have seen, created the most profound dissatisfaction among its friends, and during the presidential campaign that followed they used every expedient and every means that human ingenuity could devise, to oppose his reëlection. All the moneyed power of the corporation itself, as well as the personal influence of its directors, stockholders, and employés, was directed to that sole end during the autumn of 1832. Newspapers were subsidized, pamphleteers employed, and so-called orators hired in every part of the country, for the single purpose of misrepresenting his actions and blackening his private and public character. All the machinery of political warfare was set in motion against him and, too often, in the most outrageous and unjustifiable manner. He was openly, repeatedly, and at every point, accused of every sin in the Table, and if it were possible to have invented a new crime at that time, he would, no doubt, have been denounced as the first criminal. But the verdict of his fellow-citizens, so absolutely pronounced, was unmistakably in his favor; and, with additional reasons for the repression of a corporation that could use its power so basely, he thus alludes to it in his message:

"Such measures as are within the reach of the Secretary of the Treasury have been taken, to enable him to judge whether the public deposits in that institution may be regarded as entirely safe; but as his limited power may prove inadequate to this object, I recommend the subject to the attention of Congress, under the firm belief that it is worthy their serious investigation. An inquiry into the transactions of the institution, embracing the branches as well as the principal bank, seems called for by the credit which is given throughout the country to many serious charges impeaching its character, and which, if true, may justly excite the apprehension that it is no longer a safe depository of the money of the people."

The other matter referred to in this important document was one that had lately presented itself in a new and menacing form to the public, and which has almost as much interest for this generation as for the past. South Carolina, ever an unruly sister in the family of States, not content with opposing a protective tariff by her representatives in Congress, proceeded to organize a practical opposition to the collection of revenue in her ports, or in other words, to nullify the laws of the Union. In allusion to this illegal manifestation the President said:

"It is my painful duty to state, that, in one quarter of the United States, opposition to the revenue laws has risen to a height which threatens to thwart their execution, if not to endanger the integrity of the Union. Whatever obstructions may be thrown in the way of the judicial authorities of the general government, it is hoped they will be able, peaceably, to overcome them by the prudence of their own officers, and the patriotism of the people. But should this reasonable reliance on the moderation and good sense of all portions of our fellow-citizens be disappointed, it is believed that the laws themselves are fully adequate to the suppression of such attempts as may be immediately made. Should the exigency arise, rendering the execution of the existing laws impracticable, from any cause whatever, prompt notice of it will be given to Congress, with the suggestion of such views and measures as may be deemed necessary to meet it."

For Andrew Jackson these were very mild words indeed, but they were not heeded. Previously, however, to this message of November 24th, 1832, South Carolina, having first declined all participation in the presidential contest, issued a manifesto entitled "An ordinance to nullify certain acts of the Congress of the United States, purporting to be laws laying duties and imposts on the importations of foreign commodities." The following is a fair sample of this extraordinary *pronunciamiento:*

"We, therefore, the people of the State of South Carolina, in convention assembled, do declare and ordain, and it is hereby declared and ordained, that the several acts and parts of acts of the Congress of the United States, purporting to be laws for the imposing of duties and imposts on the importation of foreign commodities, and now having actual operation and effect within the United States, and more especially, an act entitled 'An act in alteration of the several acts imposing duties on imports,' approved on the nineteenth day of May, one thousand eight hundred and twenty eight, and also an act entitled 'An act to alter and amend the several acts imposing duties on imports,' approved on the fourteenth day of July, one thousand eight hundred and thirty-two, are unauthorized by the constitution of the United States, and violate the true meaning and intent thereof, and are null, void, and no law, nor binding upon this State, its officers or citizens; and all promises, contracts, and obligations, made or entered into, or to be made or entered into, with purpose to secure the duties imposed by the said acts, and all judicial proceedings which shall be hereafter had in affirmance thereof, are and shall be held utterly null and void."

To all this and much more of the same

character, President Jackson replied at great length in a proclamation of remarkable temper, force, clarity of reason, and profound knowledge of the nature and spirit of our institutions, and the relation between a State and the Federal Government. He concluded that remarkable state paper in the following language, which should be read and re-read by every citizen of this Republic:

"I adjure you, as you honor their memory; as you love the cause of freedom, to which they dedicated their lives; as you prize the peace of your country, the lives of its best citizens, and your own fair fame, to retrace your steps. Snatch from the archives of your State the disorganizing edict of its convention; bid its members to reassemble, and promulgate the decided expressions of your will to remain in the path which alone can conduct you to safety, prosperity, and honor. Tell them that, compared to disunion, all other evils are light, because that brings with it an accumulation of all. Declare that you will never take the field unless the star-spangled banner of your country shall float over you; that you will not be stigmatized when dead, and dishonored and scorned while you live, as the authors of the first attack on the constitution of your country. Its destroyers you cannot be. You may disturb its peace, you may interrupt the course of its prosperity, you may cloud its reputation for stability, but its tranquillity will be restored, its prosperity will return, and the stain upon its national character will be transferred, and remain an eternal blot on the memory of those who caused the disorder.

"Fellow-citizens of the United States, the threat of unhallowed disunion, the names of those, once respected, by whom it is uttered, the array of military force to support it, denote the approach of a crisis in our affairs, on which the continuance of our unexampled prosperity, our political existence, and perhaps that of all free governments, may depend. The conjuncture demanded a free, a full, and explicit enunciation, not only of my intentions, but of my principles of action; and, as the claim was asserted of a right by a State to annul the laws of the Union, and even to secede from it at pleasure, a frank exposition of my opinions in relation to the origin and form of our government, and the construction I give to the instrument by which it was created, seemed to be proper. Having the fullest confidence in the justness of the legal and constitutional opinion of my duties, which has been expressed, I rely, with equal confidence, on your undivided support in my determination to execute the laws, to preserve the Union by all constitutional means, to arrest, if possible, by moderate, but firm measures, the necessity of a recourse to force; and, if it be the will of heaven that the recurrence of its primeval curse on man for the shedding of a brother's blood should fall upon our land, that it be not called down by any offensive act on the part of the United States."

Early in January, 1833, the President sent a message to Congress embodying the principles laid down in his proclamation, and informing that body of all the steps taken by the nullifiers of South Carolina. He asked for additional legislation, and expressed " his confident reliance upon the disposition of each department of the government to perform its duty and to coöperate in all measures necessary in the present emergency," declaring, at the same time, his determination to preserve " the integrity of the Union " and to execute the laws by all constitutional means. The firm attitude thus assumed by Jackson had the desired effect, for the time being at least, and the Compromise bill, introduced by Mr. Clay in May, and passed with the assistance of Mr. Calhoun, gave to the people of his fiery State a decent pretext for withdrawing from a position no longer tenable. Secession, however, was not destroyed, but postponed; the snake was scotched, not killed, as we of this day know to our sorrow and cost.

The thirty-second Congress assembled on the 2d of December, 1833, and received the President's message; the first since he had entered on his second term. In it he alluded to the prosperous state of the public finances and to other matters of general interest, but the salient point was still the condition of the United States Bank. It now became evident to every one that the war between the Executive, or rather the democratic party, and that institution, was to be fought to the bitter end. He thus alludes to it:

"Since the last adjournment of Congress, the Secretary of the Treasury has directed the money of the United States to be deposited in certain State banks designated by him, and he will immediately lay before you his reasons for this direction. I concur with him entirely in the view he has taken of the subject; and, some months before the removal, I urged upon the department the propriety of taking that step. The near approach of the day on which the charter will expire, as well as the conduct of the bank, appeared to me to call for this measure upon the high considerations of public interest and public duty. The extent of its misconduct, however, although known to be great, was not at that time fully developed by proof. It was not until late in the month of August, that I received from the government directors an official report, establishing beyond question that this great and powerful institution had been actively engaged in attempting to influence the elections of the public officers by means of its money." The news of the removal of the government deposits was made subsequently, in a communication to Congress by Mr. Taney, Secretary of the Treasury.

The excitement in and out of Congress caused by the appearance of those two documents was intense. In the Senate the opposition were led by Webster, Clay, and Calhoun; Benton, as usual, leading the democratic forces. Resolutions of condemnation of the President's course in withdrawing the deposits were introduced, and, after a protracted and able debate, were carried by twenty-six yeas to twenty nays. President Jackson replied to them in a "protest" marked by great ability and good temper. This again led to some violent remarks in the Senate, and a notice of motion by Benton to expunge the objectionable resolutions. But on the suggestion of Mr. Pointdexter the protest was not only not received but declared to be a breach of the privileges of that body.

Such was the temper of the upper house when the next session opened in December, 1834. After alluding to the French spoliation difficulty, and declaring the country "free from public debt, at peace with all the world, and with no complicated interests to consult in our intercourse with foreign powers," the President returned with renewed vigor to the attack on the United States Bank. He accused it of causing the confiscation of $170,041, dividends on the public stock, and of creating the recent commercial distress by "locking up" money and refusing to discount the notes of merchants, or accommodate, as was the former custom, State banks and other like moneyed institutions; and concluded by saying:

"I feel it my duty to recommend to you that a law be passed authorizing the sale of the public stock; that the provision of the charter requiring the receipt of notes of the bank in payment of public dues, shall, in accordance with the power reserved to Congress in the 14th section of the charter, be suspended until the bank pays to the treasury the dividend withheld; and that all laws connecting the government or its officers with the bank, directly or indirectly, be repealed; and that the institution be left hereafter to its own resources and means."

The debates on the French Spoliation bill, as it was called, occupied the greater portion of the time of Congress during this session, but the general distress, or as we would now call it, the panic, and the affairs of the bank, were the prevailing topics among the people. Indeed so thoroughly was the popular mind stirred up by newspapers and demagogues that men seemed driven to frenzy. The President himself nearly fell a victim to this insane spirit. On the 30th of January, 1835, while he was coming out of the capitol, attended by two members of the cabinet, he was confronted by a man, who evidently had been lying in wait for him, and who, at the distance of eight feet, deliberately presented a pistol to his face and attempted to fire it off. The cap only exploded, and the would-be asssasin drew another pistol, but with like result. Jackson, with his old fire, raised his cane and rushed on the miscreant, but before he could reach him the man was knocked down by a lieutenant of the Navy and quickly secured by the spectators. He proved to be an Englishman named Lawrence, and though imprisoned, escaped any adequate punishment, on the plea of insanity. The most curious circumstance connected with this affair was, that the pistols, upon examination, were found to be in good order and were easily discharged on the first attempt to do so.

At this session also, Mr. King of Alabama presented resolutions of that State requesting the expunging of the resolutions of censure from the journal of the Senate, but they were laid on the table by a vote of twenty-seven to twenty. Benton also introduced his promised resolution to the same effect, but it met a similar fate.

The President's message to the twenty-fourth Congress, which commenced its sittings in December, 1835, contained nothing of special importance, being taken up almost wholly by discussions on our relations with France, and some domestic questions of minor importance. Only a passing allusion is made to the United States bank, which had some time previously made an assignment. The sad condition of its affairs then became apparent, and more than justified the attacks of its opponents.

The expunging resolutions were again introduced by Benton, but deferred, and meanwhile the presidential election took place which resulted in the election of Van Buren, Jackson's candidate and personal favorite, by a vote of one hundred and seventy, to seventy-three for Gen. Harrison and twenty-six for Mr. Hugh L. White.

This in itself was a triumph for the outgoing president, a substantial indorsement of his policy, and a victory for his party, the fruits of which, however, were thrown away in the next four years, when the helm of the ship of state was no longer in his firm grasp.

The last message of the venerable president to the session of 1836-'7, was altogether occupied by financial matters and the condition of the Indians, and was only remarkable for its plain, touching, and even pathetic peroration; when the great statesman, having reached the term allotted to man, borne down by the weight of years and long and faithful services, loaded with honors and crowned by the applause of millions of freemen, was about to relinquish the authority of chief magistrate and, descending into the ranks of private citizenship, to await in composure that grand, final end, which comes alike to prince and peasant.

"Having now finished," he said, "the observations deemed proper on this, the the last occasion I shall have of communicating with the two houses of Congress at their meeting, I cannot omit an expression of the gratitude which is due to the great body of my fellow-citizens, in whose partiality and indulgence I have found encouragement and support in the many difficult and trying scenes through which it has been my lot to pass during my public career. Though deeply sensible that my exertions have not been crowned with a success corresponding to the degree of favor bestowed upon me, I am sure that they will be considered as having been directed by an earnest desire to promote the good of my country; and I am consoled by the persuasion that whatever errors have been committed will find a corrective in the intelligence and patriotism of those who will succeed us. All that has occurred during my administration is calculated to inspire me with increased confidence in the stability of our institutions, and should I be spared to enter upon that retirement, which is so suitable to my age and infirm health, and so much desired by me in other respects, I shall not cease to invoke that beneficent Being to whose providence we are already so signally indebted for the continuance of his blessings on our beloved country."

It was during this session that Benton again introduced his expunging resolutions, which, after a long and exciting forensic contest in which that distinguished senator bore more than the lion's share, were passed on the 16th of March, 1837, by a vote of twenty-four votes for the measure to nineteen against it, five members being absent. The great majority of the people applauded the act, and President Andrew Jackson, in consequence, retired from his great office and laid down the authority which he had exercised for eight years without a stain on his private or public character.

Previous to retiring into private life, Jackson, after the example of Washington, issued an address to the American people, full of fatherly advice and patriotic sentiments, and with almost prophetic vision he, amongst other things said :

"What have you to gain by division and

dissension? Delude not yourselves with the belief, that a breach, once made, may be afterwards repaired. If the Union is once severed, the line of separation will grow wider and wider; and the controversies which are now debated and settled in the halls of legislation, will then be tried in fields of battle and determined by the sword. Neither should you deceive yourselves with the hope that the first line of separation would be the permanent one, and that nothing but harmony and concord would be found in the new associations formed upon the dissolution of this Union. Local interests would still be found there, and unchastened ambition. And if the recollection of common dangers, in which the people of these United States stood side by side against the common foe—the memory of victories won by their united valor; the prosperity and happiness they have enjoyed under the present constitution; the proud name they bear as citzens of this great republic—if all these recollections and proofs of common interest are not strong enough to bind us together as one people, what tie will hold united the new divisions of empire, when these bonds have been broken and this Union dissevered? The first line of separation would not last for a single generation; new fragments would be torn off; new leaders would spring up; and this great and glorious republic would soon be broken into a multitude of petty States, without commerce, without credit; jealous of one another; armed for mutual aggressions; loaded with taxes to pay armies and leaders; seeking aid against each other from foreign powers; insulted and trampled upon by the nations of Europe; until, harassed with conflicts, and humbled and debased in spirit, they would be ready to submit to the absolute dominion of any military adventurer, and to surrender their liberty for the sake of repose. It is impossible to look on the consequences that would inevitably follow the destruction of this government, and not feel indignant when we hear cold calculations about the value of the Union, and have so constantly before us a line of conduct so well calculated to weaken its ties."

We have dwelt more at length on President Jackson's domestic policy, because there were issues involved in it, some of which, though settled, had a direct and important bearing on the future welfare and prosperity of the country; and others are still subjects of discussion between the two great political parties who claim the suffrages of the people. His foreign diplomacy, however, was almost equally important; was conducted in his wonted straightforward style; was equally successful, and had a most beneficial result on the recognition of our rights as a nation as well as our commercial interests at home and abroad. We have already mentioned his opening a direct and unrestricted trade with the British West Indies; to this may be added the French indemnity treaty, by which our citizens obtained from that government five millions of dollars "for unlawful seizures, captures, etc., of their vessels, cargoes, or other property;" the Danish treaty, and the Neapolitan,

Portuguese, and Spanish indemnity treaties, by which our citizens' claims against those countries, so long in dispute, were fully and satisfactorily settled. The history of the commercial treaty with Russia, the most important of all, is thus briefly sketched by Mr. Benton:

"Up to the commencement of General Jackson's administration there was no American treaty of amity, commerce, and navigation with that great power. The attention of President Jackson was early directed to this anomalous point; and Mr. John Randolph of Roanoke, then retired from Congress, was induced, by the earnest persuasions of the President, and his Secretary of State, Mr. Van Buren, to accept the place of envoy extraordinary and minister plenipotentiary to the Court of St. Petersburg—to renew the applications for the treaty which had so long been made in vain. Repairing to that post, Mr. Randolph found that the rigors of a Russian climate were too severe for the texture of his fragile constitution; and was soon recalled at his own request. Mr. James Buchanan, of Pennsylvania, was then appointed in his place; and by him the long-desired treaty was concluded, December, 1832—the Count Nesselrode, the Russian negotiator, and the Emperor Nicholas the reigning sovereign. It was a treaty of great moment to the United States; for, although it added nothing to the commercial privileges actually enjoyed, yet it gave stability to their enjoyment; and so imparted confidence to the enterprise of merchants. It was limited to seven years' duration, but with a clause of indefinite continuance, subject to termination upon one year's notice from either party. Near twenty years have elapsed: no notice for its termination has ever been given; and the commerce between the two countries feels all the advantages resulting from stability and national guarantees. And thus was obtained, in the first term of General Jackson's administration, an important treaty with a great power, which all previous administrations and the Congress of the Confederation had been unable to obtain."

The treaty of friendship and commerce with the Ottoman Porte, ratified in 1830-'1, was next in importance. By the terms of this agreement our trade with the Turkish dominions was placed on the footing of the most favored nation; and being without limitation as to time, may be considered as perpetual, subject only to be abrogated by war, in itself improbable, or by other events not to be expected. The right of passing the Dardanelles and of navigating the Black Sea was secured to our merchant ships, in ballast or with cargo, and to carry the products of the United States and of the Ottoman empire, except the prohibited articles. The flag of the United States was to be respected. Factors, or commercial brokers, of any religion, were allowed to be employed by our merchants. Consuls were placed on a footing of security, and travelling with passports was protected. Fairness and justice in suits and litigations were provided for. In questions between a citizen of the United States and a subject of the Sublime Porte, the parties were not to be heard, nor judgment pronounced, unless the American interpreter was present. In questions between American citizens the trial was to be before the United States minister or consul. "Even when they shall have committed some offence, they shall not be arrested and put in prison by the local authorities, but shall be tried by the minister or consul, and punished according to the offence." All that was granted to other nations by the treaty of Adrianople was also granted to the United States, with the additional stipulation, to be always placed on the footing of the most favored nation—a stipulation wholly independent of the treaty exacted by Russia at Adrianople as the fruit of victories, and of itself equivalent to a full and liberal treaty; and the whole guaranteed by a particular treaty with ourselves, which make us independent of the general treaty of Adrianople. Assistance and protection were to be given throughout the Turkish dominions to American wrecked vessels and their crews; and all property recovered from a wreck was to be delivered up to the American consul of the nearest port, for the benefit of the owners. Ships of war of the two countries were to exhibit toward each other friendly and courteous conduct, and Turkish ships of war were to treat American merchant vessels with kindness and respect. This treaty has now been in force a number of years, observed with perfect good faith by each, and attended by all the good consequences expected from it. The valuable commerce of the Black Sea, and of all the Turkish ports of Asia Minor, Europe, and Africa, travelling, residence, and the pursuit of business throughout the Turkish dominions, are made as safe to our citizens as in any of the European countries.

To these may be added treaties of commerce and amity with Morocco, Siam, and the Sultan of Muscat, all of which contained conditions favorable to our merchants and travellers, and placed our trade with those powers on a most satisfactory footing.

Having thus secured to the Republic a sound and permanent position among the family of civilized and even semi-civilized nations, opened up to its enterprise and industry new channels of wealth and new marts for the sale of its fabrics and produce abroad; having at home relieved the country from a load of debt, crushed the monopolists of the United States Bank, settled as far as possible the Indian question, repressed the extravagant expenditure of public money for unnecessary improvements, stamped out secession, and modified the tariff—the United States respected abroad and on the high road to prosperity—President Jackson on the 4th of March delivered the insignia of his high office into the hands of his successor and, turning his back on the capital forever, returned to his beloved Hermitage, and to the bosom of his friends and family.

Eight years beyond the allotted threescore and ten were allowed him for rest and preparation for the final catastrophe. It would be unreasonable to suppose that all this time was spent in private concerns and social communion alone. He could not, if he would, entirely shut out the world of politics, for his home was, as it were, a temple where many puzzled or aspiring politicians repaired to consult the oracle. It is needless to say that their reception was always cordial and their visits fraught with good and wholesome advice. It was impossible, though no longer taking an active part in public affairs, that he should not feel deeply interested in everything that concerned the welfare of the country for which he had so long and so zealously toiled.

At length his end drew nigh, and found him, according to the light that was given him, fully prepared to meet it. After a short illness, and surrounded by relatives and neighbors, he expired on the 5th day of June, 1845.

Of his services, military and civil, it is almost unnecessary to speak, as the evidences of them are so indelibly impressed on the history of the Republic that the rude changes of centuries will not be able to efface them. A brave, humane, and, though untrained, a skilful soldier, he undoubtedly was, but it is as a statesman, as the embodiment of the democracy of the New World, as the champion of popular rights and the unswerving foe of tyranny, bigotry, and oppression, in all their forms, he will be best remembered and revered by posterity. His private character and disposition can best be told in the following words of one who knew him intimately for nearly half a century:

"His temper was placable as well as irascible, and his reconciliations were cordial and sincere. Of that, my own case was a signal instance. After a deadly feud, I became his confidential adviser; was offered the highest marks of his favor, and received from his dying bed a message of friendship, dictated when life was departing, and when he would have to pause for breath. There was a deep-seated vein of piety in him, unaffectedly showing itself in his reverence for divine worship, respect for the ministers of the Gospel, their hospitable reception in his house, and constant encouragement of all the pious tendencies of Mrs. Jackson.

And when they both afterwards became members of a church, it was the natural and regular result of their early and cherished feelings. He was gentle in his house, and alive to the tenderest emotions; and of this I can give an instance, greatly in contrast with his supposed character, and worth more than a long discourse in showing what that character really was. I arrived at his house one wet, chilly evening in February, and came upon him in the twilight, sitting alone before the fire, a lamb and a child between his knees. He started a little, called a servant to remove the two innocents to another room, and explained to me how it was. The child had cried because the lamb was out in the cold, and begged him to bring it in—which he had done to please the child, his adopted son, then not two years old. The ferocious man does not do that! and though Jackson had his passions and his violence, they were for men and enemies—those who stood up against him—and not for women and children, or the weak and helpless: for all whom his feelings were those of protection and support. His hospitality was active as well as cordial, embracing the worthy in every walk of life, and seeking out deserving objects to receive it, no matter how obscure. Of this I learned a characteristic instance in relation to the son of the famous Daniel Boone. The young man had come to Nashville on his father's business, to be detained some weeks, and had his lodgings at a small tavern, toward the lower part of the town. General Jackson heard of it: sought him out; found him; took him home to remain as long as his business detained him in the country, saying, 'Your father's dog should not stay in a tavern, where I have a house.' This was heart! and I had it from the young man himself, long after, when he was a State Senator of the General Assembly of Missouri, and as such nominated me for the United States Senate, at my first election, in 1820: an act of hereditary friendship, as our fathers had been early friends.

"Abhorrence of debt, public and private,

dislike of banks, and love of hard money, love of justice and love of country, were ruling passions with Jackson; and of these he gave constant evidence in all the situations of his life. Of private debts he contracted none of his own, and made any sacrifices to get out of those incurred for others. Of this he gave a signal instance, not long before the war of 1812—selling the improved part of his estate, with the best buildings of the country upon it, to pay a debt incurred in a mercantile adventure to assist a young relative; and going into log-houses in the forest to begin a new home and farm. He was living in these rude tenements when he vanquished the British at New Orleans; and, probably, a view of their conqueror's domicile would have astonished the British officers as much as their defeat had done. He was attached to his friends, and to his country, and never believed any report to the discredit of either, until compelled by proof. He would not believe in the first reports of the surrender of General Hull, and became sad and oppressed when forced to believe it. He never gave up a friend in a doubtful case, or from policy or calculation. He was a firm believer in the goodness of a superintending Providence, and in the eventual right judgment and justice of the people. I have seen him at the most desperate part of his fortunes, and never saw him waver in the belief that all would come right in the end. In the time of Cromwell he would have been a puritan."

If his eulogist had added that if he had lived in this day he would have been a Catholic, he might have been nearer the mark, for he had many of the human virtues, the exercise of which frequently precedes conversion.

CARDINAL NICHOLAS WISEMAN.

ONE of the phenomena of the age is undoubtedly the restoration of the Catholic religion in England, its growth in every part of Great Britain, and its propagation among all classes of her population since the Emancipation act of 1829. While on the Continent the ancient faith seems to superficial observers to be losing ground, even in those countries which were considered preëminently attached to it, across the Channel the Church is steadily advancing its banners and drawing its recruits from the most intellectual, most influential, and noblest of the people. "United Italy" can bear with the indecencies and rapacity of a debauched monarch; Spain be in a vortex of communistic revolution, from which there seems no outlet; and Germany can be content to lie prone under the iron heel of a would-be Teutonic Cæsar, yet the very nation that led the van in the so-called Reformation, that was one of the first to initiate proscription and persecution for conscience' sake and one of the last to lay down the carnal weapons of polemical warfare, is now fast gravitating toward the See of Rome, from which the bestiality and ferocity of the Tudors had torn her. How the England of to-day differs from the England of the last and preceding centuries! Everywhere churches are being built, monasteries and nunneries founded, schools and colleges opened, orphanages and hospitals endowed, a hierarchy in high places restored, and hundreds of priests officiating where, if discovered in the time of Elizabeth or James, they would have found that there was but a step from the sanctuary to the torture chamber, from the altar to the scaffold.

Many fortuitous and happy events have occurred to bring about so desirable a change, and many pious and learned men have labored unceasingly for the same purpose, but none with more zeal, ability, and success than the late Nicholas Wiseman, Cardinal Archbishop of Westminster. So successful have been the labors of that portion of his life devoted to the interests of Catholicity in England, and so earnestly was every moment of his time employed to win her back to her allegiance to the Apostolic See, that he may without exaggeration, in this respect at least, be called the second St. Augustine. Of him the present illustrious Pontiff truly said that he was "the man of Divine Providence for England."

Let us endeavor briefly to sketch his history, and trace, however faintly, the record of his labors and triumphs.

He was born in Seville, Spain, on the second day of August, A. D. 1802. His mother was a lady of Spanish birth and name, but of undoubted Irish descent, and his father a scion of an old County Waterford family who had settled in Spain and had became extensively engaged in commerce. We are aware that the nationality of this parent has been disputed, and that the English press and so-called "Biographical Dictionaries," though they hated the Cardinal, yet were unwilling to accord the honor of his descent to Ireland, and claim him as one of themselves. But we have the authority of those who knew him long and intimately in London, and of a near relative now living in this country, for asserting what we have above stated relative to his parentage. To argue from his patronymic that he must necessarily have been English on his father's side is to show a very lamentable knowledge of Irish history. The very section of country so long recognized as the home of his ancestors was from the first a portion of the English pale, and consequently subject to its laws, such as they were. Now by the statute of Kilkenny passed in the fifteenth century, it was made a penal offence to use an Irish name, and all natives within the jurisdiction of English law were obliged to Anglicize their names forthwith. Thus McGowan became Smith or Smithson; McShane, Jackson or Johnson; McMurrough, Murphy, and so on, to the infinite confusion and perplexity of all future antiquarians and genealogists. That the Wisemans, as claimed, may have been remotely descended from a family of that name in Essex, England, is quite possible, but except in the resemblance of the names we have no proof whatever that such was the case.

At a very early age young Wiseman had the misfortune of losing his father. A few years after, the Peninsula was invaded by the French troops, and war, with its attendant consequences, plunder and devastation, overspread the land. The colleges were of course closed and the schools discontinued. Mrs. Wiseman therefore, finding it impossible to obtain a suitable education for her son at home, resolved to take him to the land of their forefathers, hoping that there she might find an opportunity of training him, according to the usages of his family, in the Catholic faith and doctrine.

In this, however, she was sadly disappointed. The dark shadow of the penal laws still hung over Ireland, and her people had not yet been aroused from their thraldom of centuries, by the trumpet tones of the great Emancipator's voice. Maynooth College, it is true, existed, mainly on a miserable stipend grudgingly and niggardly granted annually by the English government for its own good reasons, but primary education of a Catholic character was still in its infancy.

In 1810, after allowing her son to remain a couple of years at a boarding-school in the vicinity of the city of Waterford, Mrs. Wiseman brought him to England and placed him in St. Cuthbert's College, Ushaw, near Durham. The great inducement for selecting this place in preference to others seems to have arisen from the circumstance that at that time the vice-president and actual head of the college was Dr. Lingard, the author of the "Catholic History of England," then in the zenith of his fame, as he is to-day the only English author upon whose statements regarding the history of his country any reliance can be placed.

That the fond and earnest mother made a wise selection there can be no doubt, for we have it on the testimony of the cardinal himself many years after the death of the learned doctor. "I have retained upon my memory," he wrote, in his "History of the Last Four Popes," "the vivid recollection of specific acts of thoughtful and delicate kindness, which showed a tender heart, mindful of its duties amidst the many harassing occupations just devolved on him through the death of the president and his own literary engagements; for he was reconducting his first great work through the press. But though he went from college soon after, and I later left the country, and saw him not again for fifteen years, yet there grew up an indirect understanding first, and by degrees a correspondence and an intimacy which continued to the close of his life."

Here he remained for eight years, studying diligently all that could be taught him in class, and devoting his leisure hours to cultivating an intimate acquaintance with classic art and antiquarian lore. His industry even at this early stage of life was remarkable, while his gentleness and ductility of character made him a general favorite. It was at this time, also, being satisfied that his vocation was for the priesthood, he resolved to direct his studies to that end, and even contemplated a journey to Rome at some remote period. His Latin books had awakened in him a very intense love for the Eternal City, while his reverence for all things religious created a desire to view in person the fountain-head of Catholicity. Of Rome he says: "Its history, its topography, its antiquities, had formed the bond of a little college society devoted to this queen of cities, while the dream of its longings had been the hope of one day seeing what could then only be known through hearsay, tourists, and fabulous plans."

A wish so natural and a longing so much in keeping with his tastes and habits were soon to be gratified. The English College at Rome, founded by Ina, King of Wessex, A. D. 727, was in 1818 restored by Pope Pius VII, after having been closed for many years and despoiled repeatedly during the Napoleonic wars. Young Wiseman and several other English students were selected to form its first school, and thither they were despatched shortly after the Pope's authority to open the college was made public. His arrival in Rome, with six juvenile companions, early in December, was a source of genuine pleasure to the future cardinal, and the kindly reception given him by the rector, Dr. Cradwell, made him feel perfectly at ease in his new quarters. The reverend rector, who had been appointed to take charge of the restored foundation, was not only a ripe scholar and an excellent executive officer, but was as remarkable for his affection for his pupils as for his facility in imparting to them the vast and varied knowledge with which his miind was stored.

On Christmas day following, the young student was presented to Pope Pius VII. This was to the lad a source of genuine pleasure, and a day long remembered by him with peculiar satisfaction. The venerable Pontiff, in addition to the reverence attached to his sacred office and to his many and shining personal virtues, had excited the sympathy and esteem of all Christendom by his undaunted and firm resistance to all encroachments of the civil power on the rights of the Church, as well as by his long suffering and imprisonment consequent upon his courage and fortitude. Not all the blandishments of the great Napoleon could induce him to swerve a hair's breadth from his line of duty, nor all the threats, menaces, and indignities inflicted on him by that able but unscrupulous conqueror, could move him to depart for a moment from the path in which his sainted predecessors had walked. Kings and emperors, the great and mighty of the earth, had been forced to bow down at the feet of the son of a Corsican attorney, and even to court his friendship and seek his family alliance. But the Bishop of Rome, without an army, a navy, a revenue, or even a subject, with nothing but rectitude of conscience and his implicit reliance on the assistance of his Divine Master, set his anger and power equally at defiance. And, as the result showed, he conquered: a lesson from history which may not be inaptly read by the present generation of bigots who are now engaged in prophesying the downfall of the Papacy.

The young man's interview with the sovereign Pontiff was thus subsequently described by himself: "There was the halo of a confessor round the tiara of Pius that eclipsed all gold and jewels. . . .
Instead of receiving us, as was customary, seated, the mild and amiable pontiff rose to welcome us, and meet us as we approached. He did not allow it to be a mere presentation, or a visit of ceremony. It was a fatherly reception, and in the truest sense our inauguration into the duties that awaited us. . . The friendly and almost national grasp of the hand, after due homage had been willingly paid, between the head of the Catholic Church, venerable by his very age, and a youth who had nothing even to promise; the first exhortation on entering a course of ecclesiastical study—its very inaugural discourse from him whom he believed to be the fountain of spiritual wisdom on earth; these surely formed a double tie, not to be

broken, but rather strengthened, by every subsequent experience."

Doubtless the good pope felt a peculiar gratification in welcoming those young English students and in beholding in them the germs of a great order, the inchoate laborers in the vineyard, whose services in the future would do much to bring within the pale of Catholic unity a people who at one time had given so many illustrious sons to the Church. As the Father of the Faithful he yearned for the conversion of every part of the globe, but more especially for that country that had so unaccountably and suddenly fallen into heresy and rebellion against God's authority.

As in St. Cuthbert's, Wiseman proved himself, in the English college, a student of wonderful application, patience, and versatility. His hours of regular study were employed in the most diligent manner, while the time allotted to recreation was devoted to exploring the old classic ruins, tracing the half-effaced monuments of the past, deciphering the almost obliterated mural inscriptions, and particularly in wandering through the catacombs and crypts, where the early Christians lived, worshipped, and were buried. The result of his exploration in these latter he has given us in very eloquent and concise language, in his beautiful historical tale, "Fabiola," and alludes to them frequently in his writings and lectures. In fact he never seemed tired of referring with evident gratification to, as he expresses it, "images of long, delicious strolls in musing loneliless, through the deserted ways of the ancient city; of climbing among its hills, over ruins, to reach some vantage-ground for mapping the subjacent territory, and looking beyond the glorious chains of greater and lesser mountains, clad in their imperial hues of gold and purple; and then perhaps of solemn entrance into the cool solitude of an open basilica, where the thought now rests, as the body then did, after the silent evening-prayer, and brings forward from many well-remembered nooks every local inscription, every lovely monument of art, the characteristic feature of each, or the great names with which it is associated. . . . Thus does Rome sink deep and deeper into the soul, like the dew, of which every separate drop is soft and weightless, but which still finds its way to the root of everything beneath the soil, imparting there to every future plant its own warm tint, its own balmy fragrance, and its own rejuvenescent vigor."

Such were the "hours of idleness," as spent by the future cardinal, and while others employed their vacation in mere sight-seeing or trivial amusements, his young and impressionable soul was drinking in those pure draughts of beauty and love of Christian art: and it is to those early pursuits, and the knowledge acquired through them, that the world is indebted for most of the rare sketches of ancient Roman life, topography, and art, with which so many of his lectures are adorned.

It is even questionable whether he did not carry his search after the beautiful and antique too far, at this period, for we find that of his fellow-students who accompanied him from England all or nearly all had been ordained and had returned home, and "were gaining a crown in heaven to which many of them have passed." But we must also recollect that Providence always shapes the means to the end, and, while some are destined for useful obscurity, equally meritorious, others are designed for higher and loftier actions and require peculiar and more comprehensive training and instruction. What would be of little use, in the matter of accomplishments, to a quiet, laborious priest, in the prosecution of his daily and hourly avocations, becomes a necessity to a prince of the Church, to one who would not only have to treat with the highest intellects of the outer world, but, from his position, would be obliged to govern many, as much by the grandeur of his mind as by the authority of his office.

At length, in 1825, his wishes were gratified. "The aim of years," he says, "the goal of long preparation, the longed-for crown of unwavering desires, the only prize thought worthy of being aspired to, was attained in the bright jubilee spring of Rome. It marks a blessed epoch in a life to have the grace of the priesthood superadded to the exuberant benedictions of the year." It will be remembered, 1825 was the jubilee year.

In the meantime Pius VII had passed away, and was succeeded by Leo XII, whose partiality for the inmates of the foreign colleges at Rome is well known. To him, shortly after his election, our young student was presented, and, in reply to a remark of his Holiness, he candidly replied: "I am a foreigner who came here, at the call of Pius VII, six years ago; my first patrons, Pius VII, Cardinals Litta, De Pietro, Fontana, and now Consalvi, are dead, I therefore recommend myself to your Holiness's protection, and I hope you will be a father to me at this distance from my country." Words so feeling and yet so simply expressed could not but have found their way to the tender heart of the venerable pontiff. He promised the youthful stranger his protection and kept his word faithfully during his entire reign.

Dr. Wiseman relates the following instance of his kindness soon after, speaking of himself as a third person :

"It so happened that a person connected with the English College was an aspirant to a chair in the Roman university. He had been encouraged to compete for it, on its approaching vacancy, by his professors. Having no claims of any sort, by interest or connection, he stood simply on the provision of the papal bull, which threw open all professorships to competition. It was but a secondary and obscure lectureship at best; one concerning which, it was supposed, few would busy themselves or come forward as candidates. It was, therefore, announced that this rule would be overlooked, and a person every way qualified, and of considerable reputation, would be named. The more youthful aspirant unhesitatingly solicited an audience, at which I was present. He told the Pope frankly of his intentions and of his earnest wish to have carried out, in his favor, the recent enactments of his Holiness. Nothing could be more affable, more encouraging, than Leo's reply. He expressed his delight at seeing that his regulation was not a dead letter, and that it had animated his petitioner to exertion. He assured him that he should have a fair chance, 'a clear stage and no favor,' desiring him to leave the matter in his hands.

"Time wore on; and as the only alternative given in the bull was proof, by publication of a work, of proficiency in the art or science that was to be taught, he quietly got a volume through the press—probably very heavy; but sprightliness or brilliancy was not a condition of the bull. When a vacancy arrived, it was made known, together with the announcement that it had been filled up. All seemed lost, except the honor of the pontiff, to which alone lay any appeal. Another audience was asked, and instantly granted, its motive being, of course, stated. I was again present, and shall not easily forget it. It was not necessary to re-state the case. 'I remember it all,' the Pope said most kindly; 'I have been surprised. I have sent for C——, through whom this has been done; I have ordered the appointment to be cancelled, and I have reproved him so sharply that I believe it is the reason why he is laid up to-day with fever. You have acted fairly and boldly, and you shall not lose the fruits of your industry. I will keep my word with you and the provisions of my constitution.' With the utmost graciousness he accepted the volume—now treasured by its author, into whose hands the copy has returned—acknowledged the right to preference which it had established, and assured its author of fair play.

"The Pope had, in fact, taken up earnestly the cause of his youthful appellant; instead of annoyance, he showed earnestness and kindness; and those who had passed over his pretensions with contempt were obliged to treat with him and compromise with him on terms that satisfied all his desires. Another audience for thanksgiving was kindly accorded, and I witnessed the same gentle and fatherly temper, quietly cheerful, and the same earnest sympathy with the feelings of him whose cause had been so graciously carried through. If this young client gained no new energies, gathered no strength from such repeated proofs of interest and condescension; if these did not both direct and impel, steer and fill, the sails of his little bark through many troubled waters; nay, if they did not tinge and savor his entire mental life, we may write that man soulless and incapable of any noble emotions."

In 1826, Father Wiseman was appointed vice-rector of the English College, and thus prevented from going on the home mission, and two years afterwards, when his kind preceptor was appointed bishop, he was named as his successor. He had already received the title of Doctor of Divinity, while in his twenty-second year, for having maintained a public disputation in theology with marked success.

Though still a young man, and in a city where the best intellect and most laborious students in Christendom were wont to congregate, Father Wiseman had acquired an enviable reputation, both as a theologian, an archæologist, and a linguist. He was particularly recognized as an Oriental scholar, and was in fact one of the few men in Europe at that time who had succeeded in obtaining a mastery over the elaborate and many-sided languages of the East. The publication of his " Horæ Syriacæ," his first production given to the public, confirmed the general impression, and obtained for him the professorship of Oriental languages in the Roman University in 1827, without necessitating his separation from the English College.

In the latter he taught for many years with great and well deserved success. The discipline he enforced was neither too rigid nor too lax, and the course of studies embraced as great a variety of branches as was consistent with the objects for which the institution was restored to subserve: the preparation of young ecclesiastics for the English mission, and their despatch, as soon as possible after their ordination, to the scenes of their future labors. There are many priests and even bishops yet living in Great Britain, who studied under him, and who love to acknowledge with gratitude the benefits they received from his edifying example and wise counsels. Knowing well that the popular mind of that day, as of our own, was fast gravitating toward the study of the natural sciences, and through it, when misdirected or not directed at all, into infidelity and atheism, he took particular care to have those sciences taught in his college, and to impress on the minds of his pupils that they would not only have to combat doubt and materialism in their ordinary forms, but in the more attractive, though not less insidious and dangerous garb of research into the hidden mysteries of nature. That his views of the duties of an English priest were correct is thoroughly proved by recent experience, and that he succeeded in impressing them on the minds of the students is demonstrated by the number of reverend gentlemen in England who have entered, of late years, upon the discussion of scientific matters against those who would turn the presence of God's works into an argument against his very existence.

It was in 1827 also, that Leo XII resolved

to institute in the church of Gesù e Maria, a course of lectures in English for the benefit not only of all the persons in the colleges and religious communities in Rome who understood that language, but for all others who might wish to attend them. In selecting a fitting preacher, the choice naturally fell on Dr. Wiseman, and he was forthwith selected by his Holiness. Describing the audience at which he received his commission, the Doctor afterwards wrote:

"The burden was laid there and then with peremptory kindness, by an authority that might not be gainsaid. And crushingly it pressed upon the shoulders. It would be impossible to describe the anxiety, pain, and trouble which this command cost for many years after. Nor would this be alluded to were it not to illustrate what has been kept in view in this volume—how the most insignificant life, temper, and mind may be moulded by the action of a great and almost unconscious power. Leo could not see what has been the influence of his commission, in merely dragging from the commerce with the dead to that of the living one who would gladly have confined his time to the former—from books to men, from reading to speaking. Nothing but this would have done it. Yet supposing that the providence of one's life was to be active, and in contact with the world, and one's future duties were to be in a country and in times where the most bashful may be driven to plead for his religion or his flock, surely a command overriding all inclination and forcing the will to undertake the best and only preparation for those tasks, may well be contemplated as a sacred impulse and a timely direction to a mind that wanted both. Had it not come then, it never more could have come; other bents would have soon become stiffened and unpliant; and no second opportunity could have been opened after others had satisfied the first demand."

What between his duties as rector, his professorship in the university, and the preparation and delivery of these lectures, which were always listened to with attention and criticised with no little severity by crowds of English-speaking visitors in the Eternal City, his time must have been fully employed. Yet he found leisure to compose, mainly for the benefit of his pupils, an essay on "Science and Revealed Religion," afterwards embodied in his lectures on the the same subject. Upon waiting on the Pope Pius VIII, to present a copy of this little work, he found that his Holiness had not only already read it, but honored him with the remark: "You have robbed Eygpt of its spoil, and shown that it belongs to the people of God." This criticism, coming from so high a source, must have been peculiarly gratifying to so appreciative a mind as that of Dr. Wiseman. In fact the subject was one he had constantly studied, and upon which he always loved to descant, and soon after the appearance of the essay he was induced by Cardinal Weld to prepare a course of lectures on the "Connection between Science and Revealed Religion," which were delivered, first in his own college and afterwards in the Cardinal's apartments, to a select and distinguished auditory.

As the facilities for publishing these lectures in Rome, in the language in which they were delivered, were very limited, Dr. Wiseman resolved to visit England and supervise their publication there. He accordingly went to that country, and had the satisfaction of finding this, what may be called his first effort to popularize a theme so long a concealed one for the masses, highly successful. The appearance of his book was the signal, of course, for violent attacks from all quarters antagonistic to Catholicity and to Christianity, but the more intelligent and better class of the people read and admired it, and even the "scientists" could not help admitting its vast erudition and cogency of argument. Many a doubting mind, lost in the mazes of scientific speculation, has been set right and restored to sound Christian views by the perusal of those philosophic, yet perfectly comprehensible lectures. During his visit he also preached a number of discourses of a controversial character, during the Advent of 1835, in the Sardinian Chapel, London; and another series, during the following Lent, in St. Mary's Church, Moorfields. These latter were subsequently published, under the title of "Lectures on the Principal Doctrines and Practices of the Catholic Church"; while the former gave rise to an animated controversy between him and Dr. Turton, afterwards Protestant bishop of Ely, on the subject of the Holy Eucharist. The temper and courtesy displayed on both sides on this occasion were admirable, and produced a profound impression on the English public favorable to the Catholics, though it was generally admitted that the Anglican divine, no mean opponent, had been vanquished by the superior learning and higher moral argument of the Roman Doctor. In 1836, he returned to Rome, to his college and his beloved studies. But the events of the preceding decade had to a great extent changed the direction of his mind and aroused in his bosom a latent desire which had long slumbered there. This was a longing for the reconversion of England, and an ardent hope that he might be thought worthy to become a participant in that holy work. While at St. Cuthbert's his young heart panted for the sights and scenes of old Rome; to kneel at the shrines of the saints and worship God in the magnificent and awe-inspiring basilicas which adorn the capital of Christendom; to tread the stones made sacred by the blood of the early martyrs, and explore the dungeons and hiding-places of the primitive Christians, were his highest ambition, and his dearest wish on earth. Now, in the plenitude of his manhood, his mind fully developed and enriched with all the learning of his sacred profession and the acquirements of an accomplished scholar, he yearned to return to the land of his boyhood and to offer at her feet all the treasures of his great soul, if by so doing he could win even the least of her children to the knowledge of the Faith.

Many circumstances combined to intensify this feeling. He had, years previously, opened a correspondence with his old teacher, Dr. Lingard, who sought to impress on him the necessity of having additional clergymen in England, consequent on the increased demands for clerical ministration arising out of Irish Catholic immigration to the large cities and manufacturing centres. Then, his former students, who were now hard at work at home, would write to the same effect. Next came the rumor, faint at first, that "popery" had invaded the Gibraltar of Anglicanism, Oxford University, and that the ablest thinkers in that time-honored seat of learning were gravitating toward Rome. This was followed by his lectures in the Gesù e Maria, at which not only Catholics but Protestants of all sects attended, and which drew around him a host of English friends most desirous for his presence in London. His subsequent visit to England, and his cordial and respectful reception there, seem to have finally determined him to put into execution the project that had so long haunted his thoughts.

Four years' probation were still to be spent in the Christian capital before he could consider himself qualified to undertake the ponderous and difficult task he proposed to himself. During these years most of the time he could spare from his assigned duties were spent in consultation at the side of the then Pope, Gregory XVI, from whom, as from his predecessors, he received much valuable advice and every mark of confidence and esteem. In his "Four Last Popes" he gives the following striking picture of his visits to that pontiff:

"An embrace would supply the place of

ceremonious forms on entrance. At one time a long, familiar conversation, seated side by side; at another a visit to the penetralia of the pontifical apartment (a small suite of entresols, communicating by an internal staircase) occupied the time. . . What it has been my happiness to hear from him in such visits, it would be betraying a sacred trust to reveal; but many and many words there spoken rise to the mind in times of trouble, like stars, not only bright in themselves, but all the brighter in their reflection from the brightness of their mirror. They have been words of mastery and spell over after events, promises, and prognostics which have not failed, assurances and supports that have never come to naught."

At length the long anticipated change took place. In 1840 it was resolved to increase the number of vicars apostolic in England to eight, instead of four, to meet the demands of the growing Catholic population. Dr. Wiseman was thereupon nominated coadjutor to the Rt. Rev. Dr. Walsh at

Wolverhampton, and was consecrated that year in Rome by Cardinal Fransoni. He left that city immediately after, to the great regret of the many friends to whom he was so long and so intimately known, and, if we may judge from his own account, the feeling was amply reciprocated.

"It was a sorrowful evening," he writes, "at the beginning of autumn, when, after a residence in Rome prolonged through twenty-two years, till affection clung to every old stone there like the moss that grew into it, this strong but tender tie was cut, and much of future happiness had to be invested in the mournful recollections of the past."

Shortly after his arrival in England Bishop Wiseman, in addition to his duties as vicar apostolic, assumed the presidency of St. Mary's College, Oscott, near Birmingham, and, profiting by his large experience in the English college, he introduced into that institution many important changes, which had the effect of increasing its efficiency and establishing it as one of the first seminaries in the United Kingdoms.

From this period may be dated Bishop Wiseman's actual entrance into active, real life. His previous labors had been but a source of training necessary to fit him for the discharge of higher and more responsible duties. Heretofore he had spent his life in the society of learned men or in the quietude of his study; there was no venal press to spew forth its daily or weekly venom, no hireling demagogues to excite the passions of the mob against the professors of the ancient faith, no parliamentary zealot to forge and utter the vilest calumnies against the Church and her faithful ministers. All these agencies of evil he was now about to encounter, and, if possible, to live them down. How well and faithfully he wrought out his great mission, and how completely he silenced, if he did not annihilate, his opponents and the enemies of the Church, we shall see presently.

The Catholics of England thirty-five years ago occupied a strange and by no means an encouraging position. They consisted of four widely distinct and to some extent antagonistic elements. These were:

I. A few noble families who had clung to the faith through all changes and vicissitude, and had succeeded in retaining, by one device or another, a portion, at least, of their ancient patrimony.

II. French *émigrés*, with their descendants, who had not returned to their native country at the Restoration, but had settled down and married in England.

III. Isolated groups of Catholic gentry and farmers, mostly in the north, whose ancestors had remained faithful to the Church, despite the cruel barbarity of the penal days, or who, from their comparative insignificance, had escaped the blood-hounds of the law.

IV. Irish emigrants and their children, who from choice or necessity had left their native land to seek employment in the sister island, and, who, with the tenacity of their race, clung with increased fondness to the sole consolation of their exile—the Catholic religion. This class far outnumbered all the others combined, as they also surpassed them in the fervor of their devotion and the singleness of their purpose; but being strangers and generally poor, they had little social standing and less political power. They were to be found in the greatest numbers in London, Liverpool, Leeds, Manchester, Birmingham, and other manufacturing cities, but seldom in the smaller towns or rural districts.

There was unfortunately little cohesion among these classes, and nothing that might be called a unity of action or a disposition to labor together for a common cause. There was no literature, worthy of the name, to disseminate correct opinions on religion, morality, or civil polity; few literary institutions or semi-benevolent societies to bring together persons of divers walks in life; in fact, no common channel for the flow of common ideas or any recognized captains to defend the persecuted faith and the outraged rights of the entire body. Again, there were no recognized hierarchy, few priests in proportion to the work to be done, but a few schools, and those of doubtful usefulness, and not many monasteries, nunneries, or hospitals like those which now dot the face of the country.

To correct all these evils and supply so many defects was the gigantic task allotted to the future cardinal.

But, in addition to the active coöperation of the priesthood and the zealous support of some influential laymen, Dr. Wiseman soon found assistance in a quarter from which it was least expected. This was the "Tractarian Movement," as it was then called. At first springing up among the Anglican professors in Oxford for the avowed purpose of correcting the errors and reconciling the incongruities of the Church of England, it ended in producing some of the brightest, purest, and most profound prelates and preachers of the faith in England. As Dr. Wiseman took a great interest in that movement, a short sketch of its origin and development may not be out of place here.

Its birth may be dated from 1832, at Oxford University, where a number of young but thoroughly trained fellows and students had been long in the habit of assembling in friendly intercourse and discussing various points of Anglican doctrine and discipline. Principal among these was Dr. John Henry Newman, and his companions, Hurrell Froude, John Keble, Hugh Rose, and Dr. Pusey. As Dr. Newman was the leading spirit of the new school and the most advanced mind, we quote from his "Apologia pro Vita Sua" some passages descriptive of the peculiar notions, designs, and ultimate conversion of himself and many of his friends.

After describing a tour he made on the Continent in 1832-'3, his visiting Catholic countries, churches, and shrines, and his calls upon "Monseigneur (Cardinal) Wiseman at the Colligio Inglese" in Rome, he says:

"When I got home from abroad, I found that already a movement had commenced in opposition to the specific danger which at that time was threatening the religion of the nation and its Church. Several zealous and able men had united their counsels, and were in correspondence with each other. The principal of these were Mr. Keble, Hurrell Froude, who had reached home long before me, Mr. William Palmer of Dublin and Worcester college, Mr. Arthur Percival, and Mr. Hugh Rose."

These gentlemen and some of their old college associates commenced the publication of a series of tracts, ninety in all, on various topics affecting the condition of the Church of England, which, from their intrinsic literary merit and novelty of opinions, attracted general attention and excited much comment and discussion. But as Dr. Newman was the recognized leader, we will let him speak for the others. He says:

"I have spoken of my firm confidence in my position; and now let me state more definitely what the position was which I took up, and the propositions about which I was so confident. These were three: 1. First was the principle of dogma: my battle was with liberalism; by liberalism I meant the anti-dogmatic principle and its developments. This was the first point on which I was certain. Here I make a remark: persistence in a given belief is no sufficient test of its truth; but departure from it is at least a slur upon the man who has felt so certain about it. In proportion then as I had in 1832 a strong persuasion in beliefs which I have since given up, so far a sort of guilt attaches to me, not only for that vain confidence, but for my multiform conduct in consequence of it. But here I have the satisfaction of feeling that I have nothing to retract, and nothing to repent of. The main principle of the Movement is as dear to me now as it ever was. I have changed in many things: in this I have not. From the age of fifteen, dogma has been the fundamental principle of my religion: I know no other religion; I cannot enter into the idea of any other sort of religion; religion, as a mere sentiment, is to me a dream and a mockery. As well can there be filial love without the fact of a father, as devotion without the fact of a Supreme Being. What I held in 1816, I held in 1833, and I hold in 1864. Please God, I shall hold it to the end. Even when I was under Dr. Whately's influence, I had no temptation to be less zealous for the great dogmas of the faith, and at various times I used to resist such trains of thought on his part, as seemed to me (rightly or wrongly) to obscure them. Such was the fundamental principle of the Movement of 1833."

Again he writes:

"A cry was heard on all sides of us, that the Tracts and the writings of the Fathers would lead us to become Catholics, before we were aware of it. This was loudly expressed by members of the Evangelical party, who in 1836 had joined us in making a protest in Convocation against a memorable appointment of the Prime Minister. These clergymen even then avowed their desire that the next time they were brought up to Oxford to give a vote, it might be in order to put down the Popery of the Movement. There was another reason still, and quite as important. Monseigneur Wiseman, with the acuteness and zeal which might be expected from that great Prelate, had anticipated what was coming, had returned to England in 1836, had delivered lectures in London on the doctrines of Catholicism, and created an impression through the country, shared in by ourselves, that we had for our opponents in controversy, not only our brethren, but our hereditary foes. These were the circumstances which led to my publication of 'The Prophetical office of the Church viewed relatively to Romanism and Popular Protestantism.'"

. . . .

" I have said already that, though the object of the Movement was to withstand the Liberalism of the day, I found and felt this could not be done by mere negatives. It was necessary for us to have a positive Church theory erected on a definite basis. This took me to the great Anglican divines ; and then of course I found at once that it was impossible to form any such theory, without cutting across the teaching of the Church of Rome. Thus came in the Roman controversy.

"When I first turned myself to it, I had neither doubt on the subject, nor suspicion that doubt would ever come upon me. It was in this state of mind that I began to read up Bellarmine on the one hand, and numberless Anglican writers on the other. But I soon found, as others had found before me, that it was a tangled and manifold controversy, difficult to master, more difficult to put out of hand with neatness and precision. It was easy to make points, not easy to sum up and settle. It was not easy to find a clear issue for the dispute, and still less by a logical process to decide it in favor of Anglicanism. This difficulty, however, had no tendency whatever to harass or perplex me: it was a matter not of conviction."

While in this state of mind, an article by Dr. Wiseman, entitled the "Anglican Claim," appeared in the *Dublin Review*. A copy was put into Newman's hands, with a view to his answering it, but the impression it produced on him was far from satisfactory, for he tells us:

" I became excited at the view thus opened upon me. I was just starting on a round of visits; and I mentioned my state of mind to two most intimate friends: I think to no others. After a while I got calm, and at length the vivid impression upon my imagination faded away. What I thought about it on reflection, I will attempt to describe presently. I had to determine its logical value, and its bearing upon my duty. Meanwhile, so far as this was certain—I had seen the shadow of a hand upon the wall. It was clear that I had a good deal to learn on the question of the Churches, and that perhaps some new light was coming upon me. He who has seen a ghost, cannot be as if he had never seen it. The heavens had opened and closed again. The thought for the moment had been, 'The Church of Rome will be found right after all;' and then it had vanished. My old convictions remained as before."

But it would seem that the Doctor's convictions, if the same as before, were considerably shaken, nay, actually undermined and tottering, for he says further on, in reference to his reply:

"However, I had to do what I could, and what was best, under the circumstances; I found a general talk on the subject of the article in the *Dublin Review;* and, if it had affected me, it was not wonderful that it affected others also. As to myself I felt no kind of certainty that the argument in it was conclusive."

Thus distracted by doubts, and endeavoring in vain to find a resting-place in the bosom of the English church, Dr. Newman continued to fight even against his own convictions till he, like so many other Oxford men, overpowered by the facts and arguments that came crowding on him, abandoned the unequal combat, and became a Catholic. In 1845, in answer, he says, to "a very gracious letter of congratulation," he wrote the following letter, evidently addressed to Dr. Wiseman:

"I hope you will have anticipated, before I express it, the great gratification which I received from your Eminence's letter. That gratification, however, was tempered by the apprehension, that kind and anxious well-wishers at a distance attach more importance to my step than really belongs to it. To me, indeed, personally it is of course an inestimable gain: but persons and things look great at a distance, which are not so when seen close; and, did your Eminence know me, you would see that I was one, about whom there has been far more talk for good and bad than he deserves, and about whose movements far more expectation has been raised than the event will justify.

"As I never, I do trust, aimed at anything else than obedience to my own sense of right, and have been magnified into the leader of a party without my wishing it or acting as such, so now, much as I may wish to the contrary, and earnestly as I may labor (as is my duty) to minister in a humble way to the Catholic Church, yet my powers will, I fear, disappoint the expectations of both my own friends, and of those who pray for the peace of Jerusalem.

"If I might ask of your Eminence a favor, it is that you would kindly moderate those anticipations. Would it were in my power to do, what I do not aspire to do! At present certainly I cannot look forward to the future, and, though it would be a good work if I could persuade others to do as I have done, yet it seems as if I had quite enough to do in thinking of myself."

A short time after the despatch of this letter, Bishop Wiseman called on the writer of it, and invited him, with several other converts, to Oscott, and eventually sent him to Rome.

Dr. Newman's services in the cause of religion and Catholic literature since his conversion and ordination are too well known and appreciated in both hemispheres to need even a passing mention. His powerful defence of the Church, her doctrines and discipline, have drawn many amiable and erudite men within her sheltering arms, but his example has probably had a much greater effect, particularly on the class of thinkers from which he himself sprung. How far we may claim credit for Dr. Wiseman in securing this happy acquisition to the cause of Catholicity, it is impossible to determine, but certain it is that his writings and discourses were not without their effect on the conscientious, but troubled, minds of the Oxford men.

Two years after his advent in England, Bishop Wiseman published his letters on "Catholic Unity," and in 1849, he was made Vicar Apostolic of the district of London. During the whole of the intervening years he was actively employed in the midland district in discharging all the duties pertaining to his position as coadjutor. He was never idle, but, when he could possibly spare time, was to be found preaching in other districts or lecturing either to his pupils at St. Mary's or before literary societies and scientific bodies. In this manner he contrived to break down much of the unreasonable anti-catholic prejudices which then existed in and around Birmingham, and inspired the Catholics of that great business centre with a proper sense of the dignity of their position.

Dr. Wiseman, in 1850, was summoned to Rome by the Sovereign Pontiff, doubtless for consultation on Catholic affairs in England; at all events a short time after, the

Holy Father issued an Apostolic letter reëstablishing the hierarchy in that country, and by a subsequent brief appointed him Archbishop of Westminster and Cardinal. Cardinal Wiseman had the singular good fortune to have known personally five Popes, and to have enjoyed their uninterrupted patronage, respect, esteem, and confidence in a remarkable degree. From the Christmas day of 1818, when he received the blessing of Pius VII, of sainted memory, down to the day of his death, he had the happiness of being the recipient of every attention and kindness from the Vatican. With our present beloved Holy Father he was an especial favorite, and to him he owed the unsolicited honor of being named Archbishop and Cardinal, the seventh in order of that rank appointed for England since the Reformation, and the first who had entered the country since the commencement of Elizabeth's reign.

The reorganization of the English hierarchy created an excitement throughout Great Britain of such intensity that it is difficult in this country, even at this not very remote period, to form a conception of it. All classes and creeds were astonished and profoundly agitated, though with different emotions. To the Catholics it was an omen of unalloyed good, a harbinger of the restoration of the old days of faith and prayer, and a guarantee that the Holy Father, involved as he was in endless difficulties, still looked on them with true parental solicitude. Protestant England was of course indignant, insulting, and even threatening. Newspapers of every shade of politics and of no politics at all, opened their batteries against the Church, and every stale calumny and musty falsehood that had slept for ages was raked up from the mire of what is called modern history and found ready vent in their columns. From the ponderous daily "organ" down to the weekly penny whistle of some remote village, the same keynote was taken up, and slanders, first invented or revamped in the metropolis, spread like circles in the water, till, weaker and weaker, they at length reached the extreme boundaries of the land. Next in volubility of denunciation of the "scarlet woman," came that class of so-called "ministers of the Lord," coarse, illiterate, and intolerant individuals, mostly Methodists, who manage to earn a precarious living by stirring up the bad passions of the ignorant colliers and navvies so numerous in England and Wales. It was through the harangues of some of these self-ordained bigots that about this time a mob was formed in the city of London which dragged through the streets and actually burned outside of its limits an effigy of the Blessed Mother of God. Magazine articles also appeared by the score, and pamphlets by the hundred, the themes of which were invariably the aggression of Rome and the danger impending over the "Establishment." Now, would any sane person believe that all this abuse, vilification, and attempts at argument arose from the fact that a few ecclesiastics, who had formerly been styled vicars apostolic, were in future to be known as bishops and archbishops, with the name of some old Catholic sees attached to their titles to point out their locality and spiritual jurisdiction?

In assuming territorial titles the bishops had interfered with no person nor violated any law of the kingdom. So the zealots in parliament set to work to frame a statute prohibiting such assumption, as dangerous to their "sovereign lady the Queen, defender of the faith, etc." This bill was entitled "The Ecclesiastical Titles Act," and prohibited, under certain pains and penalties, the use in writing or otherwise by "foreign" churchmen, of English titles. It never occurred to those wise law-makers that such legislation was contrary to the terms of the Act of '29, as well as against the spirit of that much talked of and little understood conglomeration denominated the British Constitution. It answered its purpose, however, by satisfying the demand of the bigots, who now were assured that the Establishment was safe. Otherwise it was and still remains a dead letter.

It was bad enough for the Sacred College to appoint bishops and archbishops, but when it became known that to Bishop Wiseman's other high title was to be added that of Cardinal, the cup of public indignation overflowed. What, a Cardinal of the Popish Church planted in the very heart of good old Protestant England! It was too much to bear. A vicar apostolic or even an archbishop might be tolerated in the freest country on the globe, but a cardinal, never. Still what was to be done? The Catholics were too numerous to be intimidated by the mob, and acts of parliament had not been found strong enough to stem the ever-rolling tide of "papal aggression." The only remedy was, like that adopted by the lawyer who had a very bad case to defend—to abuse the opposite counsel. And this was done right roundly. Scribblers of sorts all and degrees of viciousness put their steel pens in rest and charged at the head of countless columns of mendacity and vituperation on the daring intruder from Rome. It was all to no purpose however, for the cardinal pursued the even tenor of his way, winning friends on all sides while constantly gaining souls to Christ. Some, like Newman and the Oxford men, he set thinking and searching after truth by his profound disquisitions on the doctrines and dogmas of the Church; others he led into the fold by his captivating lectures on Christian art and science, and many, who were yet in the shadow of doubt, he enlightened and convinced by his eloquence and argument in the pulpit.

He had now the highest ecclesiastical office in the three kingdoms, and he set himself diligently to work to fuse and assimilate the different classes into which the Catholics had been divided. From his arrival in England he was sensible of the low condition of Catholic literature, if it can be said that there was any literature there thirty-five years ago. He resolved to create and foster one. Good books, periodicals, and newspapers, he held to be the best supports of morality and religion. He not only pointed out the way toward acquiring those helps, but followed it himself. He collected his lectures and sermons, and published them in several volumes; he wrote a most interesting and instructive history of Popes Pius VII, Leo XII, Pius VIII, and Gregory XVI; a very beautiful classic tale, entitled "Fabiola," and "Letters on Ecclesiastical Affairs." For years he was one of the editors of the *Dublin Review*, and many of the ablest articles which appeared in that quarterly between 1840 and 1860 were the production of his pen. To the newspapers and lesser periodicals he was a liberal patron and a frequent contributor, and was always willing to aid them with his purse and advice whenever it was found expedient to do so. Though a cardinal, and having multifarious duties to perform, he was not above writing stories or sketches when a moral was to be pointed or a difficult point to be elucidated. Take, for example, his delightful little paper on the "Ancient Saints of God," published in the *Month* a short time previous to his demise. In relating the miraculous interposition of SS. Abdom and Sennen in favor of a young French officer during the siege of Rome in

1848, he thus steps aside for a moment to descant on devotion to the saints:

"But this is more than a subject of joy: it is one of admiration and consolation. For it is the natural course of things that sympathies and affections should grow less by time. We care and feel much less about the conquests of William I, or the prowess of the Black Prince, than we do about the victories of Nelson or Wellington; even Alfred is a mythical person, and Boadicea fabulous; and so it is with all nations. A steadily increasing affection and intensifying devotion (as in this case we call it) for those remote from us, in proportion as we recede from them, is as marvellous—nay, as miraculous—as would be the flowing of a stream from its source up a steep hill, deepening and widening as it rose. And such I consider this growth, through succeeding ages, of devout feeling toward those who were the root, and seem to become the crown, or flower, of the Church It is as if a beam from the sun, or a ray from a lamp, grew brighter and warmer in proportion as it darted further from its source.

"I cannot but see in this supernatural disposition, evidence of a power ruling from a higher sphere than that of *ordinary* providence, the laws of which, uniform elsewhere, are modified or even reversed when the dispensations of the gospel require it; or rather, these have their own proper and ordinary providence, the laws of which are uniform within its system. And this is one illustration, that what by every ordinary and natural course should go on diminishing, goes on increasing. But I read in this fact an evidence also of the stability and perpetuity of our faith; for a line that is ever growing thinner and thinner tends, through its extenuation, to inanition and total evanescence; whereas one that widens and extends as it advances, and becomes more solid, thereby gives earnest and proof of increasing duration.

"When we are attacked about practices, devotions, or corollaries of faith—'developments,' in other words—do we not sometimes labor needlessly to prove that we go no further than the Fathers did, and that what we do may be justified from ancient authorities? Should we not confine ourselves to showing, even without the help of antiquity, that what is attacked is good, is sound, and is holy; and then thank God that we have so much more of it than others formerly possessed? If it was right to say *Ora pro nobis* once in the day, is it not better to say it seven times a day; and if so, why not seventy times seven? The rule of forgiveness may well be the rule of seeking intercession for it. But whither am I leading you, gentle reader? I promised you a story, and I am giving you a lecture, and I fear a dry one. I must retrace my steps. I wished, therefore, merely to say that, while the saints of the Church are very naturally divided by us into three classes—holy patrons of the Church, of particular portions of it, and of its individual members—there is one raised above all others, which passes through all, composed of protectors, patrons, and nomenclators, of saints themselves. For how many Marys, how many Josephs, Peters, Johns, and Pauls, are there not in the calendar of the saints, called by those names without law of country or age!

"But beyond this general recognition of the claims of our greatest saints, one cannot but sometimes feel that the classification which I have described is carried by us too far; that a certain human dross enters into the composition of our devotion; we perhaps nationalize, or even individualize, the sympathies of those whose love is universal, like God's own, in which alone they love. We seem to fancy that St. Edward and St. Frideswida are still English; and some persons appear to have as strong an objection to one of their children bearing any but a Saxon saint's name as they have to Italian architecture. We may be quite sure that the power and interest in the whole Church have not been curtailed by the admission of others like themselves, first Christians on earth, then saints in heaven, into their blessed society; but that the friends of God belong to us all, and can and will help us, if we invoke them, with loving impartiality."

It was in this way the Cardinal by practice and precept supplied a great desideratum in English Catholic life, and the results of his labors are yet prominently to be seen in the very high order of books on religious and historical subjects which are annually issued from the Catholic press of London. He was also an earnest advocate for local organizations, when of a moral, benevolent, or literary character, and was always ready by his presence as a spectator or a lecturer to assist them in their good work. His appearance in the latter capacity before mixed audiences had an especial effect in removing many prejudices from the minds of those who had been taught to regard the Catholic as the religion of the ignorant and its ministers as the embodiment of grossness and asperity.

In the performance of the duties more particularly belonging to his position he was equally fortunate. He found, as we have said, the Catholics of England divided, without appreciable social or political influence, and to a great extent with inadequate pastoral supervision. He united them in one harmonious mass, raised them to a level, at least, with the most prominent of the sects, and left them with fourteen bishops, over fifteen hundred priests, nearly a thousand churches and chapels, more than two hundred and fifty religious communities and convents, and twenty colleges.

In 1860, the Cardinal again visited Rome, and for the last time beheld the scenes of his early youth. His reception by the Holy Father was such as might have been expected from the character of these two great soldiers of the Church. The cardinal, modest and humble as ever, knelt at the feet of the successor of St. Peter, and received his benediction; the good Pope raised him up, and embraced him with the affection of a father. Many and long were the conferences they subsequently had together, but what transpired during those interviews is, and probably will forever remain, a profound secret.

Strengthened and rejuvenated by his visit he again returned to the scene of his apostolic labors, and for four years was unremitting in his exertions. But he was now soon to be called to the reward of his many good works. "He had fought the good fight, he had kept the faith," and his day of toil was near its close. Early in 1875, his health, never very robust, showed symptoms of decay, and soon after it became known to his sorrowing friends that his days were numbered. On Saturday, February 4th, eleven days before his death, he issued a circular to the clergy of his archdiocese, requesting them to cease praying for his recovery but to pray during the Mass on the following Sunday for the grace of a happy death. On the 5th, surrounded by the canons of the chapter, he made the usual solemn asseveration of his faith, and added the following words: "I wish to express before the chapter that I have not, and never had in my whole life the very slightest doubt or hesitation as to any one of the articles of faith. I have always desired to keep it, and it is my desire to transmit it intact to my successors. *Sic me Deus adjuvat et hæc sancta Dei Evangelia.*" On the 15th of February, 1865, his spirit passed away.

His obsequies were conducted with all the solemnities known to the Church on such sad occasions, and his mortal remains were followed to their resting place in the Roman Catholic cemetery, Kensal Green, by tens of thousands of bereaved friends and mourning spiritual children.

How wonderful are the ways of Providence! In the life of Cardinal Wiseman we find a new exemplification of the inscrutable justice of the Divine Power. Here is a boy, an orphan, whose ancestors had to fly their native land for their devotion to the Catholic faith; raised up, nurtured, and trained in the centre of Christendom and sent to recall to a knowledge of God the very nation that had so cruelly persecuted his forefathers. In the early ages, Ireland sent many holy and zealous men to convert the Anglo-Saxons, but it is very doubtful if any among them were more learned, more earnest, or more successful in their mission than the illustrious bishop whose body lies mouldering without the confines of the English capital.

LIEUTENANT-GENERAL PHILIP H. SHERIDAN.

THE late civil war, which for four years desolated our country, resulting in the death or maiming of hundreds of thousands of citizens and the introduction of woe and sorrow into as many households, was not without its advantages. Apart from the political amelioration of some four millions of our fellow-beings, which grew out of the struggle as a military necessity, and the questions of inter-State and constitutional law which were finally and forever settled by the arbitrament of the sword, in the court of last resort convened on the field of battle, it awakened the dormant energies of the country and taught our citizens and the subjects of other governments our real strength and fertility of resources. It is generally conceded that war, with its usual attendants, famine and pestilence, is an evil of great magnitude, but there are misfortunes far greater that could befall a nation than even these combined. A people who from long repose yield themselves up to enervating pleasures or smother the noblest emotions of the soul in the sordid pursuit of gain cannot long remain free. Human nature appears to be so constituted that it sets little value on what comes to it unsought or which, being cheaply purchased, is indifferently estimated. Commerce, manufactures, and agriculture, are excellent things in their way, and indispensable to the greatness of a nation, but history teaches us the lesson that a community which becomes exclusively devoted to those pursuits insensibly but surely loses its virility, and eventually falls a prey to domestic tyranny or foreign aggression. Hence it is that war, providing it be waged in a just cause, becomes sometimes the lesser of two evils, if not an actual blessing. Besides, it has its positive advantages, its peculiar virtues, which are rarely to be found in times of tranquillity. It is on the field, and in defence of the helpless and the weak, that true courage is fully displayed, and it is there also that the strongest and most dis-

Sommerset in that county, is the oldest temple of worship in the State; and here young Sheridan's pious mother would often bring him to learn those solemn and salutary lessons of faith and charity which in all the trying hours of his after life were never forgotten.

Little is known of his childhood but that he was an open-hearted, ingenuous, and daring boy, fond of all the amusements natural to his age and social position, and particularly attached to the noblest of irrational animals, the horse. Many anecdotes are related of his courageous, not to say reckless, riding, and of his hairbreadth escapes with untamed animals. His father, like most emigrants burdened with a large family, was unable to give his boy as good an education as he desired, and "Phil," being of an independent turn of mind, resolved to make his own way in the world before his boyhood had well commenced. He therefore journeyed to Lanesville, Muskingum county, and when other lads of his age were enjoying the advantages of proper tuition or whiling away their time in sports and pastimes, the inchoate general was occupied in the useful but not very exalted duty of driving a water-cart. Still, in one way or another, he must have acquired the rudiments, at least, of an English education, for when about sixteen years of age, he attracted the notice of the member of Congress for his district, and was appointed through his influence a cadet at West Point; he easily passed the preliminary examination necessary for entrance into the academy. We regret that we cannot recall the name of his patron, partly in gratitude for his kindness and partly in esteem for that quickness of perception which could see in the generous, industrious young waterman the germs of great mental and physical qualities.

Nor was Sheridan unworthy of his generous benefactor. He entered the Military Academy in 1848, and graduated July 1st, 1853, "well up" in his class. McPherson, Schofield, Terrel, Sill, Hood, and other subsequently distinguished general officers,

Sommerset in that county, is the oldest temple of worship in the State; and here young Sheridan's pious mother would often bring him to learn those solemn and salutary lessons of faith and charity which in all the trying hours of his after life were never forgotten.

Little is known of his childhood but that he was an open-hearted, ingenuous, and daring boy, fond of all the amusements natural to his age and social position, and particularly attached to the noblest of irrational animals, the horse. Many anecdotes are related of his courageous, not to say reckless, riding, and of his hairbreadth escapes with untamed animals. His father, like most emigrants burdened with a large family, was unable to give his boy as good an education as he desired, and "Phil," being of an independent turn of mind, resolved to make his own way in the world before his boyhood had well commenced. He therefore journeyed to Lanesville, Muskingum county, and when other lads of his age were enjoying the advantages of proper tuition or whiling away their time in sports and pastimes, the inchoate general was occupied in the useful but not very exalted duty of driving a water-cart. Still, in one way or another, he must have acquired the rudiments, at least, of an English education, for when about sixteen years of age, he attracted the notice of the member of Congress for his district, and was appointed through his influence a cadet at West Point; he easily passed the preliminary examination necessary for entrance into the academy. We regret that we cannot recall the name of his patron, partly in gratitude for his kindness and partly in esteem for that quickness of perception which could see in the generous, industrious young waterman the germs of great mental and physical qualities.

Nor was Sheridan unworthy of his generous benefactor. He entered the Military Academy in 1848, and graduated July 1st, 1853, "well up" in his class. McPherson, Schofield, Terrel, Sill, Hood, and other subsequently distinguished general officers, being his contemporaries. All the intervening years were spent by him in the earnest, unremitting study of his future profession. Every detail of military knowledge was mastered with a quiet patience and application that astonished his more volatile fellow-students, and every duty from mounting guard upward, was performed with scrupulous fidelity. Engineering, artillery practice, cavalry and infantry tactics, languages, and all the other acquirements which form the curriculum of a West Point education, were studied with care and thoroughness. With the cadets he was a general favorite on account of his frank, manly, and straightforward disposition, while the professors of the institution regarded him as a model of industry and perseverance.

Sheridan's first commission was that of brevet second lieutenant in the First United States infantry in 1853, and in the autumn of that year we find him on duty at Fort Duncan, a military post on the Rio Grande, Texas. The station was surrounded by roving bands of Apaches, whose friendship could seldom be relied on, but whose hostility was almost certain. Of this the lieutenant was soon painfully conscious. Happening one day to wander away some distance from the fort, with but two companions, he found himself suddenly surprised and surrounded by a band of savages led by one of their most noted chiefs. The Indians, judging from the fewness of the pale faces that no resistance would be offered, called upon them to surrender; and their leader, with his followers, dismounted to disarm them. Quick as thought Sheridan vaulted into the vacant saddle and rode with all possible speed to the fort for assistance. At the moment of his arrival a company was coming out for drill, and this he straightway ordered to follow him. They arrived in time to save their comrades and chastise the Apaches; the young lieutenant with his own hand slaying the chief and some of his marauders.

An action so opportune and gallant, one would have thought, would have been rewarded with some honorable mention; but the reverse was the fact. The commanding officer of Fort Duncan never forgave him for it, and during his residence of two years made his life as uncomfortable as possible. He was a man, it appears, of violent Southern opinions, which he afterwards carried out to their logical conclusion by joining the rebellion and attempting to destroy the Government that had fed and fostered him, and to which he had more than once sworn allegiance.

In the spring of 1855, Sheridan was created a full lieutenant, and assigned to the Fourth United States infantry, then in Oregon. He accordingly proceeded to New York for the purpose of taking shipping for that State; but as the quota of recruits which he was to take to his regiment was not fully made up he was for a time placed in command of Fort Wood in New York harbor. In July he left the fort and reached the shores of the Pacific, with his men, without accident or interruption. Soon after his arrival he was ordered to escort Lieutenant Williamson's expedition to a tributary of the Columbia river, for the purpose of surveying a branch route to the Pacific railroad, and in the fall he was ordered to report at Fort Vancouver, Washington Territory. In the early spring of 1856, he accompanied Major Rains, in his campaign against the Yokima Indians, and in the battle of the Cascades, April 28th, in which those savages were completely defeated, he distinguished himself so highly that his name received special and very honorable mention in Lieutenant-General Scott's report. The result of this engagement was the formation of the Yokima Reservation, with Lieutenant Sheridan as its civil and military commandant, a position which, it seems, he filled with great credit to himself and to the satisfaction of his superior officers. The following summer he established a new military post at Yamhill. Three years of a weary and monotonous life followed, broken only by Indian skirmishes, raids, and marches through an almost deserted and impassable country. Those who have experienced the dulness and inconvenience of a soldier's life on the frontiers, deprived of everything like civilized companionship, and constantly on the alert against the attacks of wily and implacable foes, can best appreciate what a man of Sheridan's temperament and social habits must have suffered; but it was part of his duties; and, as usual, he performed it with cheerfulness and fidelity.

At length he was commissioned captain in the Thirteenth United States infantry, then commanded by Colonel (now General) William T. Sherman, and in 1861 ordered to report at Jefferson Barracks, St. Louis, Missouri. He was there first detailed as president of a board of audit to examine claims against the government alleged to have been created under Fremont during that officer's sojourn in the west. Although the position was an entirely new one to him, he acquitted himself with more than credit; for he contrived, while allowing all just demands of the claimants, to satisfy the authorities in Washington as to the equity of his decisions.

At the commencement of the war, the government very wisely assigned subordinate officers of the regular army to the more important posts and bases of supplies, as commissaries or quartermasters. The step was most judicious, for it greatly facilitated the movement, clothing, and feeding of troops. Volunteers, though of equal or perhaps superior intelligence in ordinary business transactions, had not yet acquired a sufficient knowledge of these essential requisites of a well-governed army, and required instruction from those who had been taught it as part of their profession. Thus Captain Sheridan was appointed chief Quartermaster-General to the Army of the Southwest, then in Missouri. His arrival at headquarters is thus graphically described by a staff officer: "A modest, quiet little man was our quartermaster. Yet nobody could deny the vitalizing energy and masterly force of his presence. Neat in person, courteous in demeanor, exact in the transaction of business, and most accurate in all matters appertaining to the regulations, orders, and general military customs, it was no wonder that our acting chief quartermaster should have been universally liked." In December, in the same capacity, he reported at Lebanon to General Curtis, and was immediately put on duty. The depots at Rolla and Springfield were under his charge, and his whole time was occupied in providing and forwarding rations, arms, and accoutrements to the troops. After the battle of Pea Ridge, March 6th, 1862, he was sent to Wisconsin to purchase horses, but he was soon recalled to the field, as his services at the time could not well be dispensed with, and was appointed quartermaster under Major-General Halleck. In May occurred the battle and siege of Corinth. During the latter, the necessity of an efficient cavalry force, to cut off raiders and intercept supplies, and a dashing and experienced officer to lead it, became apparent, so the choice fell on Sheridan, who was forthwith commissioned by the Governor of Minnesota, Colonel of the second Volunteer cavalry of that State.

The change must have been a pleasant one for such an enthusiastic horseman, for though the staff appointment had many attractions and comforts, the position of quartermaster or commissary, being that of a non-combatant, is seldom relished by a true soldier. Still, the experience he obtained while so acting was of great service to him afterwards, when he had an independent command. Once in the saddle, Colonel Sheridan was in his proper element. Attached to Elliott's command, sometimes with one regiment and at others with two, he was incessantly raiding round Corinth, harassing the enemy, and intercepting their convoys. On the 6th of June, being on a reconnoissance below Donaldson's Crossroads, he fell in with Forrest's cavalry, and, after a sharp engagement, drove them back in confusion. On the 8th he pursued them for several miles and chased them through Baldwin, and on the 12th, his cammand, consisting of the Second Iowa volunteers and his own regiment, was formed into a brigade. He met the rebel General Chalmers, at the head of nine regiments, in all about six thousand men, July 1st, and, with his little brigade, utterly defeated him and followed up his victory by a pursuit of twenty miles. For this gallant action he received the greatest praise in orders from General Grant, who at the same time recommended him for promotion. He was accordingly commissioned brigadier-general a few days after; and in September following he handseled his new commission by beating Colonel Faulkner near Rienzi.

Soon after this engagement his command was greatly enlarged, and made part of the Army of the Ohio. It had become apparent that Sheridan was the proper officer to lead the cavalry, and from that time forward he was employed on every occasion when skill and daring were required. When Bragg's army threatened Louisville, then badly garrisoned, he was sent to defend it, and did so with such judgment and celerity that the rebels declined to attack it:

and when the Army of the Ohio marched in the direction of Perryville, his troopers led the van of the Eleventh division. In the battle that took place in the neighborhood of that village on the 1st of October, General Sheridan was conspicuous, not only for his bravery but for the judicious manner in which he fought his men, and though he lost over four hundred killed or wounded, he, says one of his biographers "saved the Union army."

In the latter part of October of this year the Army of the Ohio was changed into that of the Cumberland, under Major-General Rosecrans; and Sheridan was appointed to the command of a division in McCook's corps, of which his command formed the right wing. Then followed the battle of Murfreesborough, one of the most hotly contested fights of the war. Sheridan of course was in the thickest part of it, struggling manfully against overpowering numbers and obstinately disputing every inch of ground. Four times in succession he repulsed Hardee's troops, and would in all probability have held his position while he had a man left, had reinforcements not been sent to enable him to assume the offensive. These were brought by General Rousseau, who thus humorously describes the condition of affairs when he came upon Sheridan. "I knew it was hell in there before I got in, but I was convinced of it when I saw Phil Sheridan, with hat in one hand and sword in the other, fighting as if he were the devil incarnate, or had a fresh indulgence from Father Tracy every five minutes." Father Tracy here mentioned, it may be remarked, was Major-General Rosecrans' chaplain, and was highly esteemed in the Army of the Cumberland, even by those who were not Catholics, for his amiability and strict attention to his clerical duties.

On the last day of the year 1862, Sheridan was promoted to the rank of Major-General, and during the winter and early spring devoted himself exclusively to the drilling and equipping of his men, varied by an occasional raid now and then to try the mettle of their horses and to keep the enemy constantly in a state of alarm. In July Rosecrans moved toward Chattanooga, and Sheridan, as part of McCook's command, took the Shelbyville road, crossed the Elk river, and captured Cowan. On this march he also had some successful skirmishes at Liberty Gap and Winchester.

About this time the following incident occurred to the Major-General, for which we are indebted to an eye-witness for a description. He says: "The belligerent in Sheridan's organization is often aroused without the stimulus of the smell of powder. In 1863, while Sheridan was encamped in Bridgeport, Alabama, he invited General George H. Thomas, then encamped at Dickford, Tennessee, to examine the works erected at Bridgeport and the preparations going on for rebuilding the bridge. At one of the way stations, the train halted for an unusually long time, and Sheridan, in asking the conductor, a great burly six-footer, the reason of the delay, met with a somewhat gruff reply. Sheridan contented himself with reproving his manner, and ordered him to proceed with the train. The conductor did not reply, and failed to obey. After waiting for a time, Sheridan sent for the conductor, and demanded to know why he had not obeyed. The fellow answered still, in a gruff manner, that he received his orders from the military superintendent only. Without giving him time to finish the insulting remark, Sheridan struck him two or three rapid blows, kicked him off the cars into the hands of a guard, and then ordered the train forward, acting as conductor on the down and return trip. This accomplished, he resumed his seat beside Thomas as if nothing unusual had occurred, and proceeded with the conversation which had been so rudely interrupted."

The battle of Chickamauga, on the 19th and 20th of September, was a long-fought and well-contested one. Sheridan's division was hotly engaged throughout the entire engagement, particularly Lytle's and Walworth's brigades, and the result was the capture of many prisoners, from five different rebel divisions whose onslaught it successively withstood, and the colors of the Twenty-fourth Alabama. In his report of the operations of his corps on this occasion, McCook said: "To Major-General Sheridan, Third division, Brigadier-General Johnson, commanding Second division, and to B. G. Davis, First division of my corps, my thanks are due for their earnest coöperation and devotion to duty. Major-General Sheridan is commended to his country."

In October the corps of Crittenden and McCook were consolidated with Granger's, and placed under the command of that officer, Major-General Sheridan still retaining his division, which had again been greatly enlarged. The battle of Lookout Mountain, Chattanooga, or Mission Ridge, was fought on the 25th of the following month, Sheridan's division, as usual, having its full share of the fighting and the glory attendant on that victory. On the 2d day of January, 1863, occurred the engagement at Stone river, in which he likewise played a conspicuous and important part.

Of this entire campaign it is enough to say that no matter in what part of the line the fiery Major-General was placed, there the hardest sort of fighting and the most desperate attacks and resistance were sure to take place, and with equal certainty the Union troops were ever the victors. Much credit of course is due to Sheridan's men for their discipline, courage, and endurance. They were the flower of the young farmers of the West and Southwest, mostly Irish by birth or extraction; but it must be remembered that the best troops in the world will make but a poor display when actually under fire, if commanded by timid or ignorant officers. In all our experience of actual warfare we have seldom found the enlisted men give way to the enemy till their officers showed signs of wavering or confusion, and we have known raw recruits to stand as firm as the oldest veterans, when their commandants have set them the example of intrepidity and coolness.

Early in 1863, Sheridan was transferred from the Southwest to the East, and a new and larger field of enterprise and distinction was opened to him. On the 9th of March Grant was summoned to Washington, commissioned Lieutenant-General, and intrusted with the command of the entire land forces of the United States. It was understood at the time, and confirmed by subsequent events, that he was to be left untrammelled in the disposition and movements of the various armies of the Union, and that he was to use his own discretion in the selection of general officers to command them; they of course looking to him in all cases for their orders and instructions. This was a wise policy on the part of the Executive and the Secretary of War, and was fully justified by the events which followed. In the exercise of this new and ample power, Lieutenant-General Grant displayed a thorough knowledge of human nature, and an insight into the mental capacity of his subordinates amounting to veritable genius. Setting aside the general officers of the old school, he selected comparatively young though not untried men for the largest and most important commands, such as Sherman, Sheridan, Thomas, Hancock, and others of that stamp, and hence the march of our troops, in whatever direction and in every portion of the country, was always attended with success.

Sheridan had spent the greater portion of February and March in Tennessee, driving out the rebels who still lingered in that State, having accomplished which he returned to Chattanooga. Shortly after his arrival he was ordered to Washington, and there, greatly to his surprise and no doubt gratification, was assigned to the command of the cavalry of the Army of the Potomac. On his way to the capital he was asked what was the object of his visit, but he could give no intelligent answer; for he did not know himself what his presence was required for. He was not then aware that Grant, during his stay in Washington, had spoken of him in the highest terms of praise, as the most capable officer to assume so important and responsible a position as that of commander of the cavalry in Virginia.

The campaign of 1864 on the Peninsula opened on the 1st of May. Major-General George Meade was in command of the Army of the Potomac, but as this was considered the most important portion of our forces, and as the fall of the rebel capital, the objective point, was much to be desired, both for its political and moral effect, Lieutenant-General Grant accompanied Meade, and remained with him till the termination of the war. Sheridan was therefore constantly under the immediate supervision and orders of the commander-in-chief.

On the 3d of May, Sheridan crossed the Rapidan river with his whole force, and on the 4th passed the Wilderness, and started on a reconnoitring and raiding expedition in the rear of the enemy. He successively visited Gray's Church, Parker's Store, and Todd's Tavern (strange names for a battle flag), Fredericksburg, Childsburg, and Beaver Dam station, and at the latter place had the good fortune to release some three hundred Union prisoners. In his course he destroyed large quantities of military stores, burned down bridges, and tore up rails by the mile. On the 11th, when within six miles of Richmond, he encountered a superior force of the enemy's cavalry under the notorious Jeb Stuart, and a desperate fight took place, ending in the death of that misguided officer with that of many of his troops, and the capture of several guns and prisoners. On the following day, he threw out a detachment toward Richmond, which passed the two outer lines of defence, reached within a mile of the city, and having obtained all necessary information, returned to the main body. His next movement was to cross the Chickahominy, but on arriving at Meadow Bridge he found it partially destroyed and impassable for artillery and cavalry, as well as defended on the other side by a large force of rebels. Nothing dismayed, he ordered his men to ford the river, and dashing across, soon put the enemy to flight. While the combat was in progress, his rear was attacked, so that he was placed between two fires. Leaving a small force to reconstruct the bridge and pursue the first party of rebels, he turned on his new assailants, and after routing them thoroughly, chased them through Mechanicsville, with the loss of many killed or wounded and several hundred prisoners. He then proceeded, carrying destruction everywhere, by Bottom's Bridge to General Butler's headquarters, having made the entire circuit of the enemy's rear in an incredibly short space of time and thoroughly effected the object of his expedition. Again we find him at headquarters at White House Landing on the Pamunky, guarding the flank of Meade's army, and in that position he rendered most essential service when Grant crossed his army over the James river, June 14th and 15th. Some conception may be formed of his valuable aid to the infantry and artillery on that occasion, when it is understood that the entire army, consisting of not less than a hundred and thirty or a hundred and forty thousand men, with their guns, wagons, horses, and cattle, crossed a broad, rapid, and deep river without losing a man, a gun, a caisson, or an ambulance, and that too, in the very face of Lee's whole army.

Petersburg now became the object of attack, as constituting the key to Richmond. Some preliminary attempts to take it having failed, Grant regularly invested the city and threw up works in front of it. Sheridan's cavalry being thus let loose, recommenced their usual tactics. Crossing the North Anna river, he advanced through Buckchild's to Gordonsville. Here he encountered a force of rebel calvary, and almost cut it into pieces. He next went to Guiney's station on the Fredericksburg and Richmond railroad, where he halted for a few days to rest his men, and thence returned to the White House. But he was soon again in motion. On the 23d and 24th, he defeated the rebels at Jones's Bridge on the Chickahominy, and at St. Mary's Church, and crossed the James river five miles above Powhattan Point. From this time until the beginning of August Sheridan may be said to have never been out of the saddle, except during the limited times he allowed himself for sleep. It has even been asserted that on many occasions he was seen taking his scanty meals on the road, his charger on a trot, and his men following close after. Whether this be true or not, he certainly performed a great deal of work by day and night and was perpetually employed on the flanks and in the rear of the enemy.

To make a diversion in favor of Lee's army, then pent up in Petersburg and Richmond, as well as to gather in or destroy the crops, a large force of rebels was sent to the fertile Shenandoah Valley, under General Early. This body, scattering over the country, obtained much plunder; and what could not be carried off was destroyed. Meeting with little opposition at first, it advanced within a few miles of Harper's Ferry, and even threatened our communications with Washington. But its successes were short-lived. On the 7th, Major-General Sheridan was assigned to the middle Military Division to oppose those incursions, and soon after we find him indulging in his pastime of skirmishing with detachments of Early's army. On the 15th of September Grant left City Point on a visit to his cavalry commander, and the result of the conference is thus laconically described by the former: "I saw," said that general, "that there were but two words of instruction necessary—'Go in.'" And Sheridan did "go in" with a vengeance, for on the 19th he attacked Early near Winchester, defeated him, left hundreds of his men dead or dying, and captured several thousand prisoners. Following up the fleeing rebels, he overtook them the following day at Fisher's Hill, routed Early again, and closely pursued his demoralized forces through Harrisonburg and Staunton.

Up to this time, Sheridan's rank in the regulars was very inferior in comparison to his merits and services; his commissions as Colonel, Brigadier-General and Major-General were only in the volunteer service, and consequently would expire as soon as the war was ended. His brilliant exploits in the Valley called the attention of the President to his abilities and immense activity in the execution of his orders, and accordingly he was appointed Brigadier-General in the regular army.

In the fall of 1864 Sheridan had occasion to visit the capital on some business of importance connected with his command, having left his troops in charge of the next ranking officer, and, as he supposed, safe from all molestation during his absence. But for once was he mistaken. The rebel general having been strongly reinforced, and having been informed by his scouts that the master spirit of the Union forces was not on the field, hazarded an attack on their position near Cedar Creek and Strasbourg on the 19th of October. The onslaught was fierce and well sustained, and at first successful, the Union troops being driven back three or four miles, defeat staring them in the face and all support far beyond assisting distance. Despair was depicted on every face. But there was succor nigher than they had anticipated. That morning Sheridan had set out leisurely for his camp, and was well on the road when he was informed of the attack. As he drew a little near to the scene of action, he recognized the fact, from the sound of the guns, that his men were falling back and the enemy was gaining ground on them. Then he plunged the rowels of his spurs into his horse's flanks and rode as few men have ridden before. What thoughts, what sensations, must have flashed through that excited brain as he tore along the road to Winchester. His own reputation imperilled, his gallant fellows defeated, and cut down, nay, perhaps the very salvation of the Republic, all, all, depending on the swiftness of his charger and his own presence in the field. On, on, he gallops, every moment seeming an hour, while the booming of the cannon sounds ominously nearer to Winchester, till at length, breathless and hatless, his horse exhausted and covered with foam, he dashes in among his disorganized troops and with a voice that penetrated from end to end of the line—a voice that had never ordered in vain—he commands a halt. The effect of his appearance and the sound of his voice were electrical. The army which had been a disorganized mass but a minute previously is now re-formed: the infantry in serried lines, the artillery in position, and the cavalry on either flank. It is now the turn of the rebels to stop in astonishment and speculate in wonder what had caused such a change in their beaten foemen. But they have not long to wait. Again the trumpet tones of Sheridan ring out clear on the atmosphere, Artillery to the front! Infantry, charge! Away they go with one long, wild cheer, every man seeming to be animated with the contagious impetuosity of his leader, as well as with a burning desire to wipe out the disgrace of defeat. The struggle was short, sharp, and decisive. The victors of the morning have become the vanquished at noon. The rebels stood firm awhile, then staggered, broke, and fled in utter confusion; and Sheridan, bareheaded but with drawn sword, led up his cavalry and completed the victory. The pursuit lasted till night, many of those who had escaped unscathed from the field fell by the road side, and those who threw down their arms, to the number of fifteen hundred, were taken prisoners. Nearly all the artillery, wagons, munitions, stores, and horses of Early's once formidable command fell into the hands of the victors, and that ill-starred general but once again troubled the peaceful valley of the Shenandoah—except, perhaps, as a reconstructed politician mourning over the "Lost Cause," or as a letter writer trying to prove that some person other than himself was responsible for his want of success. Perhaps it was "Little Phil Sheridan" who "sent him whirling down the valley." Very likely.

The decisive victory of Winchester excited the greatest enthusiasm in all quarters, and in the north, east, and west, Sheridan's name was on every tongue, and his praises resounded from one end of the Union to the other. Had our arms met with a reverse no blame could have been attached to him, for he was absent by proper authority and by orders of his superior, the President. Defeat in such a case would have been the fault of others; the glory of the day was all his own. To General Grant in particular his Major-General's splendid achievement was a source of unalloyed pleasure. He sent a communication to Washington, extolling the victor in the warmest manner; and with that disinterested admiration which he has ever felt for his subordinates, he attributed the success of the day entirely to Sheridan's personal exertions. "Turning what bid fair to be a disaster," he wrote, "into a glorious victory, stamps Sheridan, what I always thought him, one of the ablest of generals."

In addition to the thanks of a grateful country and the admiration and increased esteem of his brother officers, the hero of the Shenandoah was rewarded by the government with a commission as Major-General in the regular service, November, 1864. Thus at the early age of thirty-two, without political influence, social prestige, or family interest, the son of humble Irish parents, the errand-boy of Sommerset, found himself the second general officer in rank in the regular army of the United States, and in command higher than some who had graduated while he was driving a water-cart in the streets of Lanesville. And he had the proud satisfaction of knowing that it was to his own intrinsic capacity, to his diligence, industry, and conscientious observance of the rules of his profession, and to them alone, that he owed his success and elevation to the high grade now conferred upon him.

Sheridan left his winter quarters February 27th, 1865, took Staunton March 2d, and again defeated Early near Waynesborough. This time he left scarcely a shred of that warrior's army, and those who had the good fortune to escape hastened with their unlucky chief out of the Valley as quickly as possible, to tell the tale of their share in the "Lost Cause." As for Sheridan, who always seems to have had a passion for raiding, he turned his attention to the destruction of the railroad, the James canal, and all other means by which the rebels might endeavor to keep up their communications or forward their supplies. On the 19th of March he returned to his old quarters at White House Landing, and allowed his tired troops, weary with conquest, a few days' repose. On the 27th we find him with the main body of the army in front of Petersburg, and in two days after, at the head of nine thousand cavalry and the Fifth corps, on his way to destroy the Danville and South Side railroad.

The occupation of this road by the rebels was a vital point in their system of defence of Petersburg and Richmond, as it was the only main artery left untouched by which they could expect to get reinforcements and supplies. It was of course jealously watched and strongly guarded at all times, and when the object of Sheridan's expedition became apparent to the enemy, large reinforcements were sent to the menaced point. The contending forces met on 31st of March at Five Forks, or, as it is sometimes called, Amelia Court House. At first, victory seemed to favor the rebels, and Sheridan, with his cavalry and infantry, was obliged to fall back, but only as far as Dinwiddie, with some loss. On the following day, having been reinforced by the gallant Second corps, in which were the celebrated Irish brigade, Corcoran's Legion, Sixty-ninth Pennsylvania Volunteers, and many other battalions in whole or in greater part Irish, he again advanced to Five Forks and renewed the conflict.

This was the last battle of the war, properly so called, and it was contested on one side with all the energy, stubbornness, and courage of despair, and on the other with a fixed determination to conquer, and a cool bravery, which are the offspring only of conscious rectitude and hard-earned experience. Should the rebels succeed, they might still be able to hold their capital for months longer, and even to ask terms on condition of laying down their arms. Should they fail and the Union troops take possession of the road, Petersburg and

Richmond must be abandoned, Lee and his army would be obliged to beat an inglorious retreat, the termination of the war would become a certainty, and all the plans and hopes based on its success, would vanish like the baseless fabric of a vision.

The prize was a great one—prolonged war or speedy peace—and it was contended for on both sides with a valor commensurate with the importance of the issue involved. Sheridan was everywhere on the field during the battle, issuing orders, animating his men, and even personally putting some battalions and brigades into position under the most deadly fire. To use a familiar phrase, he was bound to win. All our troops behaved particularly well, and the Irish regiments especially, "who," to use the words of a general officer present in the engagement, "never fought so splendidly."

But the die was cast, and the days of the so-called Confederacy were numbered. As the shadows of the sinking sun lengthened on the blood-stained fields and woods of Amelia, the enemy's fire became irregular, slackened, drooped, and finally ceased, while a prolonged cheer from end to end of the lines, repeated again and again, told in unmistakable tones that the field was won. Once again the flag of the young Republic floated triumphantly over the "sacred soil" —sacred now indeed, for it contains the graves of tens of thousands of devoted Union soldiers—and the "Stars and Bars," the emblem of ingratitude, crime, and treason, sunk forever, never to be seen again but as an object of curiosity, or a warning to those who would endeavor to climb to fame and fortune on the ruins of their country.

General Grant, in writing of this battle and of Sheridan's repulse, well said: "Here Major-General Sheridan displayed great generalship. Instead of retreating with his whole command on the main army to tell the story of superior forces encountered, he deployed his cavalry on foot, leaving only mounted men enough to take charge of the horses," thus enabling him to hold his position at Dinwiddie and wait for reinforcements. The immediate results were the capture of some guns, a quantity of small arms, and over five thousand prisoners; the not very remote consequence being the evacuation of Petersburg, the surrender of Richmond, the flight of the rebel government after a diabolical attempt to fire that city, the hasty retreat of the remnant of Lee's army, and the ending of the war that had cost the country so much in blood and treasure. But Sheridan could not rest while there was remaining an armed enemy of the Republic to be found within his reach. He pursued Lee's fugitives with lightning rapidity, cut them off from their line of retreat on Staunton, and finally so hemmed them in that there was no alternative left but total and unconditional surrender. When the rebel commander offered his submission and yielded his sword to Lieutenant-General Grant under the famous apple tree at Appomattox, Sheridan was by the side of his chief, and doubtless felt that, at last, in the words formerly uttered, he had deserved well of his country.

The war was at length over, the integrity of the Union, established by our forefathers after years of struggle, suffering, and self-denial, restored, and the volunteer army, amounting to over one million of men, returned to civil life and to their anxious families. Let us pause for a moment and take a retrospective view of its origin, prosecution, and grand results, not as mere politicians or factious partisans, but as lovers of our common country who wish to profit by the dearly-bought lessons of practical warfare and desire to shield our children from the horrors of such an internecine war as many of us have witnessed in the last decade, and from the influence of which few households were exempt.

The first symptoms of secession appeared in the more conservative body of our national legislature during the first term of President Jackson. It arose out of the existence of a high protective tariff objectionable to South Carolina, and the two senators from that State, notably Mr. Calhoun, from their places in the Senate openly avowed their belief that a State had the right, under or beyond the Constitution, to nullify a law of the United States. This was followed by a convention which actually and expressly passed an ordinance of nullification, which was subsequently indorsed by the legislature. Then followed the arming, equipping, and drilling of the State militia. Mr. Clay's Compromise bill and Jackson's firmness for a time averted the danger. But Mr. Calhoun had a deeper purpose than the mere collection of revenue, as well as a deep-seated hostility to the President. His next cause of complaint was the use made of the United States mail by a few anti-slavery men of the North, and though a pronounced State Rights man he insisted that laws should be passed by certain States to suppress the anti-slavery societies. In this he again failed, and he and those who agreed with him commenced a course of speaking and writing tending greatly to exaggerate the strength and importance of the abolitionists, and thus alarm and estrange the people of the South from their brethren of the free States. In vain the representatives of these States almost unanimously protested against such statements; in vain they who ought to know best declared that the opposition to slavery where it existed was confined to an impotent and theoretical few. The virus of secession had inoculated the body politic, and it was already exhibiting symptoms of disease. The dragons' teeth were sown, and they eventually grew up armed men. In proportion as the discontent in the South increased, the anti-slavery sentiment spread in the free States, each faction feeding on the pabulum supplied by the other till so strong became the antagonistic feelings that a resort to arms was but a question of time.

Besides, another element was introduced into the struggle between the years 1840 and 1860. That was immigration, by which our new States and territories were rapidly filled up, and attained, through their representatives in Congress, a large share of legislative power and executive patronage. In a free country like ours, power always follows population, and the leaders of the South began to fear that the day was not far distant when they would be in a helpless minority in Congress. They tried to avoid this, to them impending evil, by trying to induce immigrants to settle in their section, but to no purpose, for with their peculiar system of labor white competition was impossible. The crisis at last came. The disruption of the Charleston and Baltimore democratic conventions, if not the result of a mature plan, answered the purpose of the secessionists as well, and the election of Mr. Lincoln in consequence of the division in the democratic ranks was the signal for the rupture. Thus the quarrel that had been commenced by a few fanatics on either side grew by degrees to such magnitude that it involved the middle conservative classes on both sides, and divided the country into two hostile camps. Though the conduct and language of the New England bigots cannot be defended, it is nevertheless true that the South was the aggressor and therefore wrong. It sought redress by other than constitutional means; it confiscated the public property, fired on the flag of the Republic, defied the law, and set up a quasi independent government within the United States, utterly opposed to that which it had helped to form and was so solemnly pledged to sustain.

There was no remedy left to the national authorities but to put down by armed force this formidable rebellion. But as we had been at peace for nearly half a century, excepting the short period of the Mexican war, the country was at first slow to assert its authority, and the Executive was not always fortunate in the selection of its agents. In the southwest, during the first three years of the war, much was done to restore peace and order, but in the east very little. So little indeed that when Grant commenced his campaign in the spring of 1864, the enemy held all the strong positions between Richmond and the Rappahannock river, and the Peninsula down to Fort Monroe. Long and difficult marches had been made without ceasing, sometimes over and over the same route, by the troops, and numerous bloody battles had been fought and some barren victories gained, but the fact remained uncontested that the enemy, so far from being subdued after three years' strife, were, in the winter of 1863-'4, safely encamped within a day's march of the position occupied by them in the summer of 1861, when the somewhat absurd battle of Bull Run was fought. The cause of this lamentable failure is not to be attributed to the inefficiency or want of bravery on the part of the officers of low rank and enlisted men, but to the incapacity and mutual jealousies of the generals, hardly any two of whom could agree on any particular plan or method of prosecuting a campaign. There was no unity of opinion, no concert of action, no subordination of the will to superior authority and judgment—the very life and soul of all military organizations. It was only when Grant assumed the supreme command and selected his own officers—men who knew no favoritism, and had no old grudges to satisfy—that the army of the Potomac commenced to move on uninterruptedly to victory. Cavalry officers there had been by the dozen, whose headquarters were supposed to be in the saddle, and their brains probably in the same place, who were constantly making great incursions and generally contriving to get beaten, but it was only when Sheridan took hold of this branch of the service that his horsemen learned to fight battles and win them.

The results of the successful prosecution of the war by such men were most momentous, and can only be appreciated by a consideration of what would have been the consequences, had the rebels succeeded: a humiliated people; the perpetual enslavement of four millions of human beings; a divided Republic, first into two parts and eventually into half a dozen; a second Mexico, on a larger and more enduring scale of strife and hostility; the failure of republican institutions at home, and the death-blow of liberal institutions abroad. Surely a man who by his own intrinsic merits, by his daring, courage, and admirable generalship, contributed so much as Sheridan did, deserves all the honors that a generous and admiring nation have showered upon him.

There was, however, one man then in power, whose soul was so small, or so venal, that he could not join in the general song of praise. That was Andrew Johnson, the only man that ever disgraced the presidential chair. In the spring of 1867, Major-General Sheridan was appointed to the command of the Fifth Military Division, comprising the States of Louisiana and Texas. His duties here were of a very delicate and difficult nature, but he was equal to the occasion, and performed them with great tact and determination. He facilitated as much as possible the reconstruction of that portion of the South, endeavored to win back the people to their allegiance, more by kindness and the impartial administration of justice than by force, and even went so far in the legitimate exercise of his power as to remove the provisional governors of the two States mentioned, because they were impediments to, rather than assistants of the reconstruction laws of Congress. But because he was understood to sympathize with that body in its opposition to the illegal proceedings of President Johnson, he was removed from his command in the following August, against the express wishes of General Grant, then Commander-in-Chief, who declared that Sheridan had performed his civil duties faithfully and intelligently, and earnestly protested against it. Sheridan, however, to gratify the petty malice of the accidental president, was ordered to take command of the Department of the Mississippi. He was, notwithstanding, subsequently commissioned Lieutenant-General, and is now in command of the division of the north-west with headquarters at Chicago.

Fortunately for the country, Lieutenant-General Sheridan is still alive, and after all his dangers and hardships is in robust health and likely to live many years to serve his country and even to add new laurels to the wreath already entwined round his sword. We are tempted to violate the canons of biographers of the living, which say, " Praise no man till he is dead," by a few commentaries on his private character; but knowing that this is a censorious world, and that no one is free from the accusation of flattery who speaks even less than the truth of the fortunate and meritorious, we forbear. This, however, we will say of the gallant soldier, and we have it on the authority of a clerical friend well conversant with the facts, that from the day he left West Point as a brevet second lieutenant till his acceptance at the hands of the President and Congress of the proud title he now bears, he has never for a moment forgot those good and humble parents to whom he owes his being and his first lessons in morality and religion; and that, amid all the seductions and excitement of an exceedingly active military life, he has constantly remembered them, and the teachings which they instilled into his heart in early childhood. He has at least observed that portion of the decalogue which commands us, "Honor thy father and thy mother that thy days shall be long in the land."

FIELDMARSHAL LEOPOLD O'DONNELL,

COUNT OF LUCENA AND DUKE OF TETUAN.

THERE is no family of Irish birth or extraction that has been more generally distinguished at home and abroad for high military qualities and personal nobility of conduct than that of O'Donnell, or, as it was called in mediæval history, Cinel Conaill. Other houses, like those of O'Neill, O'Brien, and O'Conor, possessed wider domains, exercised at times broader sway, and occasionally produced soldiers and statesmen of greater abilities and more enduring fame, but to the O'Donnells belongs the transcendent merit of having been ever and in all places consistent lovers of Ireland, enlightened patrons of learning, and devoted as well as practical adherents to the ancient faith. Almost without an exception, they were found on all occasions faithful even amid the faithless, and when others were willing to sacrifice the general good for the sake of private ends, or to gratify individual malice at the expense of principle, the princes of Tyrconnell invariably were found true to the national cause, literature, and religion.

For nearly eight centuries they manfully opposed by every effort in their power the Danish and Anglo-Norman invaders, with no ambition but to serve their native land, and no foe to chastise save the armed plunderers of their common country. From the time of their great ancestor Dulach, hereditary Prince of Tyrconnell (Donegal), down to the beginning of the seventeenth century, the sword of the O'Donnells scarcely ever rested in its scabbard, and while the hand of friendship was always extended to their fellow chieftains, their arm was potent to smite the native traitors as well as the foreign despoiler. As an evidence of this undying spirit of resistance to foreign aggression, we may be allowed to quote, from the historical lectures of the late Professor Eugene O'Curry, the following comments on a very old poem written by MacLonain, the laureate of Eignechan, son of Dulach, who died in 902:

"The most curious part of this poem, however, very valuable as it is in an historical point of view, is that in which we are told that the chief found himself compelled to purchase peace and exemption from plunder and devastation for his territory from the 'Danish pirates,' who were at this time committing fearful depredations along the seaboard of the island. This peace and exemption were purchased by the chief consenting to the marriage of his three beautiful daughters—Duibhlinn, Bebnadha, and Bebhin—to three of the pirate commanders, whose names were Cathais, Turgeis, and Tor. After the marriage, the pirates sailed away with their wives and their booty to Carraic Bracraighe, in Inis Eoghain, now called Innishowen. Here however the lady Duibhlinn, who had been married to the pirate chief Cathais, eloped from him while he lay asleep, taking with her a casket containing trinkets to the amount of one thousand *ungas* in gold; and she succeeded in safely making her escape to the house of Cathelan, son of Maelfabhaill, the chief of that district, who had been formerly her lover, and under whose guardianship she was the more ready to place herself. When the pirate awoke and found his bride and his casket gone, he flew in a rage to her father, and threatened to have his territory ravaged if he did not restore to him his casket. This Eignechan undertook to do; and he invited the Dane to come on a certain day, with his brother commanders, and all their immediate followers, to his court at Clann Maghain, in Donegal, where the gold should be restored, and the company royally entertained. The Danes arrived, and were well entertained accordingly; after which the company retired to the lawn of the court, where stood a tree upon which the Tyrconnellian warriors were accustomed to try their comparative strength and dexterity, and the metal and sharpness of their swords, by striking their mightiest strokes into its trunk. The company, by Eignechan's arrangement, sat in circles around this tree, for the usual purpose; the chiefs of both parties standing nearest to it. Eignechan then stood up to open the sports; and drawing his sword, he struck at the tree, but designedly missed it; the weapon glancing off with immense force, struck his reputed son-in-law, the Dane Cathais, on the head, killing him on the spot. This was a preconcerted signal for the Tyrconnellians, who instantly rushed on the rest of the band of their enemies, and quickly put them all to the sword.

"The number of Danes on this occasion may be inferred from the stated number of their ships, which was one hundred and twenty; and it is stated that not one of their crews escaped.

"Eignechan then demanded and received the casket of gold from his daughter; and he gave it all away on the spot, in proper proportions, to the tribes and to the chief churches of his principality. Just, however, as he had concluded the distribution of the whole of the piratical spoil, MacLonain, with his company of learned men and pupils, happened to arrive on the lawn, on a professional visit to his patron. And here we have a characteristic trait of the manners of the times. When the chief saw the poet, and found himself with empty hands, he blushed, and was silent; but his generous people perceiving his confusion, immediately knew the cause, and came forward to a man, placing each his part of the gold in the hands of his chief. Eignechan's face brightened; he re-divided the gold, giving the poet a share of it proportionate to his rank and profession, and disposing of the remainder among those who had so generously relieved him from his embarrassment."

The patriotism and liberality of the son of Dulach seem to have been transmitted unimpaired to his descendants. It was under their protection and patronage that the learned family of the O'Clerys, authors of the "Annals of the Four Masters," and their no less erudite ancestors flourished, two of whom, the celebrated Diarmit O'Clerigh and his son Taghg Cam, taught the lay college of the "Three Schools," of literature, history, and philosophy, as late as the fifteenth century. In 1474, Hugh Roe O'Donnell built and richly endowed the Franciscan monastery of Donegal, which existed for one hundred and twenty-seven years, shedding innumerable blessings on the surrounding population, until confiscated and dismantled in the last days of the bloody Queen Elizabeth. Of the condition of this once famous house while the O'Donnels held sway, Father Mooney, in his Latin Manuscript translated by the Rev. C. P. Meehan, says:

"Nor is it to be supposed that we lacked wherewithal to tempt the cupidity of the sacrilegious, were such to be found among the clansmen of Tyrone or Tyrconnell. Quite the contrary; for many years afterwards, when I was sacristan, no monastery in the land could make a goodlier show of gold and silver than ours. During the time I held that office, I had in my custody forty suits of vestments, many of them of cloth of gold and silver—some interwoven and brocaded with gold, the remainder silk. We had also sixteen silver chalices, which, two excepted, were washed with gold; nor should I forget two splendid ciboriums inlaid with precious stones, and every other requisite for the altars. This rich furniture was the gift of the princes of Tyrconnell; and as I said before, no matter what prey the Tyronians might lift off O'Donnell's lands, there was no one impious enough to desecrate or spoil our sacred treasury. We fed the poor, comforted them in their sorrows, educated the scions of the princely house to whom we owed everything, chronicled the achievements of their race, prayed for the souls of our founders and benefactors, chanted the divine offices day and night with great solemnity; and while thus engaged, the tide of war swept harmlessly by our hallowed walls."

Such was the happy state of this centre of piety and charity, long after the introduction of the "Reformation," in Ireland; but the wars here alluded to as harmlessly sweeping by, were simply attempts, often renewed, by Shane O'Neill, to conquer all Ulster, but who, though in many respects an unscrupulous soldier, generally venerated the temples and houses dedicated to God. The troops of the "Pale," the sanguinary apostles of English Protestantism, were less fastidious, for nothing was too sacred or too venerated to escape their brutal fury.

The last of the native princes who ruled in Donegal was Hugh Roe O'Donnell, who, in conjunction with his brother-in-law, "Aodha" (Hugh) O'Neill, waged war with the English forces for several years, sometimes with the most brilliant success; but at length, outnumbered and exhausted, was obliged to abandon the unequal struggle and retire to the Continent in 1601. Hugh Roe lived abroad several years, often the honored guest of the Sovereign Pontiffs, or at some of the Catholic courts, eventually dying at Valladolid, in Spain, where he was buried with all the ceremonies befitting his rank and faith. With him departed from Ireland forever many of the principal men of his name who had survived the war, and who, entering the service of Italy, Austria, or Spain, rose to high positions in the army and councils of their respective governments. The subsequent wars of the "Confederation of Kilkenny," and of James II, added materially to their numbers. This was particularly so in the last-named nation, where their descendants, even in our day, not only have held many of the most distinguished offices in the state, but have enjoyed social eminence and civic honors equal to those of the highest grandees of that proud and exclusive class. Their high breeding, intense catholicity, and elevated sense of honor, were thoroughly understood and appreciated by the knights of Castile and Aragon, and in turn the O'Donnells became thoroughly imbued with the hopes, aspirations, and unswerving patriotism of their adopted land, without, however, forgetting that of their ancestors and of the scene of their ancient glory.

It is a remarkable fact in the history of the Irish exiles of the last two or three hundred years, that while they were everywhere welcomed, their bravery and martial skill gladly utilized, and their services generally well rewarded by the governments under which they served, it was in Spain alone that the full measure of hospitality and reward was meted out to them, and where they were not alone honored in court and camp as wise advisers and true soldiers, but admitted into the closest family alliances. Well has the poet, addressing Ireland, said:

> Mother of soldiers! in the cause of Spain
> The Moors in Oran's trench by them were slain;
> For full a hundred years their fatal steel
> Has charged beside the lances of Castile,
> Carb'ry's, Tyrconnell's, Breffny's exiled lords
> To Spain and glory gave their gallant swords.

And Spain, of honor jealous, gave them place
Before her native sons in glory's race;
Her noblest laurels graced your soldier's head,
Her dearest daughters shared your soldier's bed:
In danger's hour she called them to the front,
And gave to them the praise who bore the brunt;
Mother of Soldiers! Spain to-day will be
A willing witness for thy sons and thee!"

From the beginning of the seventeenth century to the present time the name of O'Donnell has been a familiar one in the Spanish army lists, earning and honorably holding their commissions from the lowest to the highest grades in the service, and the subject of the present sketch may be taken as an illustration of the varied career of the entire family.

His father was Lieutenant-General Charles O'Donnell and his mother Donna Josephine Goris. While General O'Donnell was discharging the duties of Viceroy of Teneriffe, his son Leopold was born at Santa Cruz, the capital of the island, in January, 1809. From his birth he was destined for the military profession, and like the illustrious Lally Tollendal, he was trained up to the use of arms from early childhood. At the age of ten years, having, as it was supposed, completed his primary education, he was commissioned sous-lieutenant in the Spanish army known as the Imperial Alexander. This was no mere nominal appointment, no empty compliment like that so frequently paid to the infant scions of royal houses in Europe, but involved the performance of actual duties and the multifarious responsibilities of a soldier's life. In the following year, we find him at the headquarters of his regiment at Ocaña, when the so-called liberal constitution of 1812 was proclaimed by another O'Donnell, the Conde del Abisbal; but though his father and his near relatives were opposed to such a revolutionary step, and even left the service for a time, young Leopold remained at his post, and continued, with unabated ardor, the study of the profession of which he was destined to be so shining an ornament. Not without an interruption however. His mother, it seems, thinking the boy too young for the hardships and temptations of camp life, or displeased with the conduct of the temporary government, resolved to pass into France and take her son with her. For this offence of being absent without leave the little lieutenant was court-martialled on his return, but upon the hearing of the charge was honorably acquitted.

Thus we see that at an age when most boys are found at school, and their leisure time devoted to toys and the allurements of the confectioner, young Leopold O'Donnell's life had already become eventful; a foretaste of what was yet in store for him when the trying times, which were soon to desolate his country, should arrive.

When, in 1823, the French army under the Duc d'Angoulême, son of Charles X, entered Spain to support Ferdinand VII, O'Donnell was at Valladolid; and soon after we find him on the staff of the Division of Castile, as aide to the commanding general. In this capacity he was present at the siege of Ciudad Rodrigo, and so distinguished himself by intrepidity and coolness under fire that he was forthwith promoted to the rank of full lieutenant. Soon after he was commissioned captain in the royal Guards, a rank which he held up to the death of Ferdinand VII.

This latter event, which took place on the 29th of September, 1833, was the fruitful cause of all the miseries which have cursed the Spanish peninsula to the present moment—anarchy, pestilence, bloodshed, and rapine. Though commenced more than forty years ago, the civil war inaugurated by his widow Christina and Don Carlos is still raging with unabated violence on the fair plains of Aragon and in the busy towns of Catalonia, though most of the principals in the quarrel have been long since called to their great account. In order that the reader may fully understand the position of Captain O'Donnell at the commencement of hostilities we will endeavor to sketch briefly the merits of the contest.

In 1700, Charles II of Spain found himself at the point of death; and, having no issue he was unable to determine which of the numerous candidates to the succession he ought to favor. The Austrian party advocated the claims of that house, while those attached to the Bourbons were warmly in favor of one of the sons of the Dauphin of France, who was himself the child of a Spanish princess, the daughter of Philip IV. In this dilemma Charles submitted the question to Pope Innocent XII, who in turn laid it before three of the most learned and experienced of his cardinals. They, after mature deliberation, decided that "his Catholic Majesty was in conscience bound to entail the succession upon the Duc d'Anjou or the Duc de Berri, the younger sons of the Dauphin, provided proper precautions were taken against the union of the two crowns." This decision was transmitted to Charles, with an autograph letter from the Pontiff, in which he expressed his solemn concurrence, and the King, thus fortified, acted accordingly. Soon after he died, and D'Anjou became his successor under the title of Philip V.

This family alliance between France and Spain led to the long and sanguinary War of the Succession, in which England and Austria combined, without success, to drive Philip from the throne of Spain. The struggle lasted twelve years, and was ended by the treaty of Utrecht, July 13th, 1713. In that treaty it was agreed that France and Spain should forever remain under separate governments, and Philip, in compliance with its conditions, solemnly relinquished his claims on the crown of France to his brother De Berri and his heirs.

To make the matter more certain, however, he resolved to limit the succession to the Spanish throne in the male line. The project of the monarch was laid before the Councils of State and of Castile, and having been duly considered was unanimously approved by them. The Deputies of the Cortes were then in session in Madrid, and, by order of the king, letters were sent to every privileged city and town on the 10th of May, 1713, instructing them to send their delegates "full and sufficient powers to confer and deliberate upon this subject." The law limiting the succession to the male line was then duly and legally passed, and hence the introduction of what is called the "Salic law" into the Spanish constitution. In 1789, the Cortes, at the instigation, it is said, of Count Floridablanca, minister of Charles IV, petitioned that sovereign to declare by pragmatic sanction the abrogation of the law of 1713 and a return to "the old law of succession." For some reason Charles neglected to comply with the prayer of the petition, and it was only in 1830, forty years afterwards, that Ferdinand VII issued his decree which commenced as follows: "Pragmatic sanction having the force of law, decreed by King Charles IV, on the petition of the Cortes for the year 1789, and ordered to be published by his reigning majesty (Ferdinand VII) for the perpetual observance of Law 2, title 15, partida 2, establishing the regular succession of the crown of Spain."

Hitherto the existence of this law No. 2, etc., had been unknown to the Spanish public, and it soon became apparent that Ferdinand had some object in thus doing away with the Salic law. It was this: the king had been married to three wives in succession, all of whom had died without leaving issue. He therefore resolved to marry a fourth, and selected Christina of Naples. The wedding took place on the 11th of December, 1829. Two daughters were the result of this union, the older of whom, Isabel, was destined by her vacillating father and ambitious mother to fill the throne of Spain. As long as the Salic law was in existence no female could occupy this position, and consequently the succession would devolve on Ferdinand's brother, Don Carlos, and next, to his sons, of whom he had three then living. The king, therefore, influenced doubtless by his aspiring consort, determined to remove this obstruction to his daughter's elevation, and though in 1832, during a fit of sickness, he annulled the decree of 1830, he no sooner recovered than, having previously appointed the Queen Regent, he authorized the nullification of his previous act. " His royal mind having been taken by surprise," said the Queen Regent's decree of December, 1832, "in moments of agony to which he had been brought by a serious malady, he signed a decree repealing the pragmatic sanction of March 29th, 1830, which is hereafter to be held as void and of no effect." Early in 1833, Ferdinand assumed the reins of government again, and one of his first acts was to summon the Cortes to swear allegiance to the Infanta, which was accordingly done on the 20th of June, only three months before the death of Ferdinand, which occurred on the 29th of September, 1833.

The issue was now made up, and civil war was inevitable. Those in power, headed by the Regent Christina, held possession on the authority of the decrees of 1789, 1830, and December, 1832; while Don Carlos claimed the throne on the ground that the Cortes of 1789 had no power to repeal the constitutional provision of 1713, as it had been summoned for one specific purpose, to swear allegiance to the then heir-apparent, and as he himself was born one year before that time and enjoyed inchoate vested rights to the throne, neither the act of the Cortes nor the pragmatic sanction of Ferdinand could deprive him of them. With the former were the so-called Liberals and the communistic element; with the Carlists, most of the nobility and the old officers of the army, and, doubtless, the great majority of the rural population, particularly in the northern provinces. A quadruple treaty was also effected against Don Carlos, and Dom Miguel, an aspirant for the throne of Portugal, between that country, France, England, and Christina, by which it was agreed that while France was to guard her frontiers against the entry of Don Carlos's adherents into Spain, and, if required, send an army into that country to assist the Christinos, England was to keep watch and ward by sea; and all were to operate in their several ways against the Carlists and Miguelites.

O'Donnell, doubtless for good reasons, took the side of the queen, though his brother, looking on Don Carlos, or Charles

V, as the rightful monarch, espoused his cause and fought with great bravery and distinction in his army. We have seen that Leopold was captain of the Guards previous to Ferdinand's demise; immediately on the commencement of hostilities he was placed in command of a force of grenadiers forming part of a brigade to which was assigned the defence of the five principal cities of Aragon then menaced by the insurgents of Navarre. In this position his conduct was considered so meritorious, that he was speedily promoted to a higher command. We next hear of him in the defiles of Mendigorria, Arcos, Guerarra, Echerarri, and Erice, where he was severely wounded while leading his men to a charge; and it was doubtless for this act of gallantry that he was gazetted the 1st of January, 1836, as colonel of the regiment of infantry of Gerona. When able again to take the field he was placed in command of a brigade, consisting of his own regiment and that of Malorca, with which he took possession of the valley of the Err and Roncesvalles, driving the enemy before him in all directions.

Soon after, O'Donnell was sent, with his brigade and a regiment of cavalry, to the borders of Navarre, to protect the flank of the queen's army and keep open its communications with Madrid, and in doing so he had an opportunity of taking a prominent part in the battle of Unza, March 19th, 1836, for which he received his commission as brigadier-general. From June, 1836, to May of the following year General O'Donnell was obliged to keep away from active operations, in consequence of ill health and typhus fever. His enforced leisure was spent in Vittoria and Logroño. No sooner, however, had he recovered from fever than, against the earnest remonstrances of his physicians, for his wound was still unhealed, he again took the field, and having joined the headquarters of the army at San Sebastian, he was permitted to take part in the capture of the lines of Oriamenti, the surrender of Hernani, and the fall of Turenterrabia. In other respects he also did good service; for, some of the queen's regiments having about this time mutinied, he quickly reduced them to obedience, as much by his personal influence and popularity as by any display of force. This happily effected, he turned his attention to the Carlists, whom he compelled to evacuate Urrieta and Anoain, and on December 27th he was promoted major-general.

Early in the following year he occupied the defensive lines of San Sebastian, in front of the fortified towns of Hernani, Artegaraga, Oyarzun, Irun, and Tuenterrabia, besides twenty redoubts mounted with cannon. On the 24th of June he fought the enemy and drove them across the Oria, after having abandoned their works on the left bank of the river. On the 27th he again defeated them at Oyarzun, capturing many prisoners and valuable stores, and early in October he entered the city as a conqueror.

In 1839, O'Donnell was appointed to the central army in the place of Nogueras, and captain-general of the kingdoms of Aragon,

Valentia, and Murcia. The enemies' strongholds were then in Lower Aragon, in the Maistrazzo and in the provinces of Castellon, Teruel, Valencia, and Cuenca. To those places his early attention was directed, and before the close of the campaign he had taken and destroyed nearly all the hostile forts and works, and routed or captured their defenders. He found time also to relieve Lucena, then only defended by two thousand troops; and, with but eleven battalions and nine hundred horse, to signally defeat General Don Ramon Cabrera, one of the ablest and most experienced officers on either side. For this brilliant victory he was rewarded with the rank of Lieutenant-General and the title of Count of Lucena.

Thus, though twenty years a soldier, he had not attained his thirtieth year before he had won, by his skill, prudence, and desperate bravery, a military command and a reputation second to none of his countrymen. It is interesting also to recollect that a portion, at least, of his success was due to the gallantry and proverbial bravery of the countrymen of his ancestors, though we are by no means inclined to applaud the motives which induced so many Irishmen at this juncture to leave their homes and take part in the domestic quarrels of a country that had ever been friendly to them, merely to subserve the designs of a disreputable British minister.

When England entered into the quadruple alliance of 1834, she stipulated only for the employment of a naval force, but with her usual duplicity, what she dared not do openly, she endeavored to effect by subterfuge. By an order in Council, dated June 9th, 1835, the Foreign Enlistment act was suspended and Colonel Evans, himself, unfortunately, an Irishman, was selected as the instrument to draw his countrymen into the meshes of a foreign dispute, in which they could by no possibility be concerned, nor from the results of which could they be in any way the gainers. The so-called "British" Legion was however raised, not one in a hundred of the men being British, and sent out to

Spain. During most of their period of service they formed a portion of O'Donnell's command, and of course fought with desperate and headlong valor, all of which, in the newspapers of the day and even in subsequent histories, being set down to the credit of "British heroism" but, as might have been expected, their treatment by friends and foes alike was anything but flattering. By the Christinos they were regarded as mere mercenaries, and by the Carlists as adventurers who were entitled neither to quarter nor the slightest honors of war. England, too, though conniving at their enlistment, refused them all protection, and the remnant of those who had not been slain in open battle or fallen sacrifices to the aroused vengeance of the Carlist peasantry, was led homeward by an officer named O'Connell—destitute alike of honor, glory, and even of the common necessaries of life. Tom Steele, the afterwards famous Pacificator of the Repeal agitation, was, we believe, among those unfortunates, and it is, probably, to the experience acquired by him in Spain that we are indebted for his subsequent devotion to the "moral force" doctrine.

The civil war ended in 1840; the Carlist leaders were driven out of the country, and their followers either in their graves or seeking refuge in the mountains and caves. The natural results of such internecine struggles now began to show themselves. The victors commenced to quarrel over the spoils. One of the first that felt the effects of the new order of things was the Count of Lucena. Becoming dissatisfied with the intrigues of the court of the Queen Regent, he joined an insurrectionary party in Madrid in 1841, and having proceeded from thence to Pampeluna he was threatened by overpowering numbers of the government troops and compelled to seek safety in flight. By this rash act he also lost his rank in the army. In two years afterwards he returned to Spain, drove Espartero from power, and was not only restored to his rank of Lieutenant-General, but was appointed Captain-General of Cuba, the duties of which position he discharged to the satisfaction of the people of that beautiful island and the home government, till 1848. His executive abilities while in that position were as conspicuous as was his military skill during the war; and it may be said of him, what cannot be truthfully alleged of many of his predecessors and successors, that he endeavored to the best of his power to govern the Cubans with justice and moderation.

On his return home he took his seat in the Altæ Camarilla, and as a peaceful legislator promised to become even a more useful member of the body politic of Spain than he had been as an active defender of the throne on the field of battle. Many of his speeches during his parliamentary career, though short, were full of pith and good sense, and exhibited an intimacy with the intricacies of Spanish politics scarcely to be expected from one of his profession. But the affairs of Spain were fast degenerating into mere chaos, and the only remedy, if it can be called so, was armed insurrection. The disease of the grand old country had become chronic, and there was no peaceful cure that could be applied with effect. An insurrection accordingly took place in 1854, headed by O'Donnell, who, having been joined by the "Progresistas," demanded the reëstablishment of the Constitution of 1837, the dismissal of the ministry, the banishment of Christina, and the reorganization of the national guard. All this was conceded, and Espartero returned from exile to act as regent for the young queen and form a new ministry, in which the Count of Lucena held the portfolio of War.

Two years afterwards, this ministry was dissolved, Espartero again sent into banishment, and O'Donnell occupied the post of Prime-Minister from July to October, 1856. Then came his time to relinquish office, but he was again restored in June, 1858.

In 1856 O'Donnell had been created a Fieldmarshal of Spain, and when the war between that country and Morocco broke out in 1859, he, as the highest ranking officer in the army, as well as the ablest military leader, was appointed to the command of the army of invasion. Though the war lasted only one year, it was full of glory and success to the Spanish arms. In a strange country, beset with difficulties and discouragement at every step, and confronted by a brave, keen, and watchful foe, his campaign was one series of successes, so that even his enemies could not help admiring his audacity, tact, and indomitable perseverance. A peace most advantageous to Spain was concluded in 1860, and the conqueror returned amid the applause of a proud and grateful people, having, as he hoped, conferred honor on his country and race, and in return received the title of Duke of Tetuan.

But alas! for the uncertainty of political life and the inconstancy of rulers, particularly where there is no Salic law; the cheers of the populace had scarcely subsided and the favors of the court had not yet grown stale, when he again found himself an exile, and for the last time, for he died at Biarritz, France, in 1867, in the fifty-ninth year of his age, almost within sight of that country which he had served for almost half a century.

His death created a deep sensation in Spain; and those who had been most active in causing his banishment now vied with each other in honoring his memory. His remains were brought to Madrid by order of the queen, and with regal pomp and gorgeous ceremony deposited in the convent of Atocha. As he left no male issue, his title and estates descend to his nephew, Charles O'Donnell, Marquis of Altisnera.

Whatever may be our opinions of his merits as a statesman, or the correctness of his judgment as a politician, few will deny Fieldmarshal O'Donnell the possession of the leading qualities of a great and successful soldier: comprehensiveness, resolution, undaunted moral and physical courage, and a thorough mastery of the details of the art of war. With each step of promotion, from the very lowest to the highest rank, his mind seems to have risen equal, if not superior, to each new demand upon its attention, and the result was that whether called upon to act as sub-lieutenant, colonel, or general, he was always singularly prompt and invariably successful. In personal appearance he had also many advantages, having been considered remarkably handsome, even in his declining years, with a commanding figure and a stature considerably over six feet. Under other circumstances, he might have stood on the hills of Donegal or have been inaugurated at Kilmacrenan as no unworthy representative of the long line of illustrious princes of the Cinel Conaill.

THE END.

www.ingramcontent.com/pod-product-compliance
Lightning Source LLC
Chambersburg PA
CBHW031330230426
43670CB00006B/293